To

# 50 Commandments
## to
## Transform Your Life

Dr. Randall K. Hartman

ISBN: 153075772X
ISBN-13: 978-1530757725

# DEDICATION

For the men of Chapman Hall in the school year 1972-1973.

# CONTENTS

# ACKNOWLEDGMENTS

I am grateful to Olivet Nazarene University located in Bourbonnais, Illinois for providing the campus where I met Tom Drake and the other men of Chapman Hall in the fall of 1972. My life would not be the same without the friendships forged in those important years.

I am indebted to Deborah Coppenger Drake for sending me the list Tom, her late husband, left behind in his briefcase. I still have that copy and treasure it.

My highest thanks goes to Jacquie, my wife of 41 years, who always knew I would write a book. Indeed, this book would have never been written without her encouragement, insight, cajoling, and refusal to let me give up. Everyone who reads *Tom's List* owes her a note of thanks.

# PREFACE: FOUR COMPELLING REASONS YOU NEED TO READ *TOM'S LIST*

You might be tempted not to read this book. It's a free country. But with freedom comes the opportunity to make right and wrong choices. The right choice is to read and digest this book. These truths are powerful; inviting you to transform your life.

Here are four reasons why you must read this book.

1. The list is an amazing collection of the best truths gleaned from reading more than 2,000 of the top books released over the last 40 years.

Suppose someone gave you the assignment to read 2,000 books and make a list of the top 50 truths you discovered in those books. I can hear the groan coming up out of your gut. Who would want that assignment? But here's the thing: That work has already been done. Even though his life ended early, Tom Drake completed that assignment.

Many readers will not have had the privilege of knowing Tom. Let me just say that Tom would not waste his time on a truth if it did not have life-changing potential. Your task is to take these discovered truths and apply them to your life.

2. It's a way for you to make a personal statement that you are going to do something to improve your life.

How do I say this delicately? You and I aren't getting any younger: of course you already knew that! Time is slipping away. Now is the time to start upgrading your life. If you are happy with all areas of your life then maybe *Tom's List* isn't for you.

But honestly, my life needs improvement. I need to change. What about you? Now is the time for a life upgrade. Decide you are not going to be one of those people who just lets life happen.

3. *Tom's List* is a simple way to upgrade your life.

It's amazing how many people make New Year's resolutions that disappear by the end of January. As the weeks of the new year slide by, those resolutions become buried under a mound of good intentions.

One of the really hard parts in upgrading your life is to figure out how to work on the change consistently as the weeks go by. How do you make yourself work on those improvements week after week? Make the commitment to read one chapter each week. Spend the week putting that truth into practice. If you follow this plan, your life will be different.

4. The list will force you to examine areas of your life that need improvement that you have chosen to ignore.

Items on the list will be presented each week in the same order as on the original list. As I studied the list I recognized the truths seemed to be grouped together according to subject. That means you will spend several weeks working on the family and then on to another subject.

I don't know about you but there are areas in my life I tend to ignore when it comes to improvement. It's easy to turn a blind eye toward things that might make you uncomfortable or are not that interesting. *Tom's List* will force you to take a look at areas needing improvement which you often ignore.

# INTRODUCTION: HOW IT ALL STARTED

In the fall of 1972 the planets and stars aligned on the campus of Olivet Nazarene College, a small school south of Chicago. On that day of destiny, college freshmen were busy moving into dormitories while moms and dads assumed the role of heavy-breathing pack mules as they carried clothes, bedding, and other assorted treasures into tiny rooms resembling a slight upgrade from a prison cell.

It was on that day that Tom Drake came into my life.

He was one of many students I met that day along with Rick, Gary, Steve, Larry, Sid, Dave, and Louie, just to name a few. Before the month was out we became inseparable friends. We ate together, lived together, got rowdy together, and once in a while went to class together. By the end of our four-year journey, we had completed our tour of duty and became lifelong friends. To this day, when we get together, it is as if we are transported back to the early 1970s.

It amazes me to think of the life path each of us took. One became a preacher. Another became a counselor for troubled children. Several became business owners. Tom went on to become a successful businessman serving as vice president of a corporation in Indianapolis.

He married his college sweetheart and had two children. The church he attended benefited from his ability to lead people. He taught a thriving Sunday School class. Some of the young men in his class claimed Tom as their mentor as he poured his life into them.

We kept in contact across the years. Once in a while I would get an email from him indicating he would be in my area for business and "Could we do coffee?" One of the first questions Tom always asked was: "What are you reading?" The question did not surprise me. Soon after college graduation Tom made it his goal to read one book each week. Imagine reading more than 50 new books each year!

Tom did things right. He was a great family man. He loved God and served his church. When it came to business, he excelled. And as you can tell, he was an avid lifelong learner. Tom's only fault, in the judgment of this Chicago Bears fan, was that he cheered tirelessly for the Green Bay Packers.

In November 2012, he sent an email informing me he had cancer. In typical Tom fashion he announced being ready for the fight. He started a blog to chronicle his battle. The updates were sporadic. Several weeks went by, and I noticed Tom was no longer writing the updates. This was a troubling development. Word began to spread of a scheduled surgery which promised to be long and difficult.

Surgery confirmed the seriousness of his situation. He fought to recover but started to fade.

One Sunday morning after church I got in my car and made the four-hour drive to the hospital. When I arrived he was barely able to respond. I prayed with him and said goodbye. The next day, January 14, 2013, my good friend Tom died. I had lost one of my best friends. Everyone who knew him grieved the loss of someone who had made such a positive impact upon his or her life.

About three weeks later, I received a letter in the mail from Tom's wife, Deb. The brief letter thanked me for coming to the hospital. But there was more. Inside I found a neatly typed sheet of paper. Deb explained that while cleaning out his briefcase she stumbled upon a sheet of paper which contained a list of 50 truths to live by. Each truth was a one-liner. She thought I might find the list interesting. In my hands I held a copy of the original. At the top of the sheet I saw the words: "Personal Commandments."

Carefully, I read the list of Tom's Personal Commandments. It dawned on me what I held in my hands. The sheet of paper contained a distillation of meaningful truths Tom had gleaned while reading one book per week during his 40 years of reading. If you do the math, this list contained the greatest life lessons pulled out of more than 2,000 books.

This was not a list of casual suggestions. Here was a life-changing list distilled from the top books of our day, dripping with the promise of a better tomorrow, for all who applied the truths. Here were the commandments by which Tom had successfully navigated his life. It was Tom's list.

My purpose in writing this book is to share with you these truths discovered by Tom that he lived out. Each chapter will focus on the truths as listed on that sheet of paper.

Not every truth will apply to every reader. But I am convinced of one thing: If you come along for the journey, and apply the truths that speak to you, your life will never be the same.

Tom was a Baby Boomer who refused to live an ordinary life. He had figured out how to live an extraordinary life. With his list of 50 commandments to live by, you too can live beyond the ordinary.

*Tom's List* just might change your life. And there's no better way for Tom Drake to be remembered.

Disclaimer: These commandments are derived from books Tom read. I do not have the titles of these books so I cannot give any credit to the authors. But there is no intent on my part to infringe upon any copyrights held by the authors.

# CHAPTER 1: BE THE KIND OF MAN I WANT MY SON TO BE

I had to have it. Why? I'm not sure but maybe it's because I am an early adopter. But all I knew for certain was the Commodore VIC-20 sitting on the shelf had to go home with me. I suspect, like your first kiss, you always remember your first personal home computer.

For the next year, my son made the puny computer do amazing things. Following guidelines in magazines, he typed character after character of Basic computer code, creating games.

Today my son works for the University of Cincinnati as Software Development Lead. He confided in me his love of computers goes back to his exposure to the lowly VIC-20. I didn't know it then, but my early adopter love of computers rubbed off on him.

As parents, we often forget our kids scrutinize our behavior. Be honest. We would rather not think about it. Somewhere on the inside we try to convince ourselves we can be great parents by telling them what to do instead of setting a good example.

But hold on. If your parents told you what to do, but were horrible role models, it did not mean you were prison bound. My own dad was an alcoholic and drug addict, and should have spent serious time in prison. But that did not keep me from striving to rise above his example. And yet, I suspect some of the things I still struggle with are a result of how Dad raised me.

Here is what I wonder: How would my life be different if my dad had chosen to "be the kind of man" he wanted me to be?

Forty years ago Harry Chapin recorded a haunting song entitled "Cat's in the Cradle." In the song a dad tells the story of being too busy to spend time with his son. Even though his son asks him to spend time with him, Dad is just too busy. As the song progresses the dad grows old and the son moves away. The father calls the son and wants to get together with him but the son is now the one offering excuses. He just doesn't have time for dad.

Embracing this first commandment in *Tom's List* is to embrace the responsibility of parenthood. Dad and Mom, you have been entrusted with the high privilege of raising your kids. This challenge starts by owning the truth that you influence your kids far more than you realize. As a parent you should work hard to be the person you want your kid to become.

This is a startling thought. If we want our children to grow up and be good adults, we should work on ourselves. It is a counterintuitive thought. Normally we approach parenthood with the idea that raising good kids means giving them the right education, teaching them good manners, and instilling in them a good work ethic. But this first commandment on the list reminds us of a far greater truth: To have great kids, work more on yourself than on them.

What kind of adults do you want your kids to be? Kind? Loving? Educated? Thoughtful? Spiritual? When your kids are grown and raising your grandkids, how do you hope they turned out?

Here's the real question: What must you do to ensure your kids see these qualities in you? What do you need to start doing or stop doing? What do you need to let go or embrace? Make a list and act on it. And as the years go by, watch your kids become the kind of adults you wanted them to become.

Apply this to your life:

1. Look at your own life and see if you have any qualities that mirrors your parents.

2. In what ways have you turned out to be like your mom and dad?

3. Regardless of your children's age, what change can you make in your life now to impact them in a positive way?

# CHAPTER 2: LIVE LIFE FULL THROTTLE

"How fast will it go?" At 17 years of age, that question gripped me as I looked at my beautiful new 1972 Honda 175cc motorcycle. Have you noticed that teens rarely ask the "adult" question: "Is it safe to find out?"

But at that moment all I wanted to know was: "How fast?" I knew how to find out. Finding a straight stretch of highway, I opened the throttle and tightened my grip. At 90 miles per hour the engine topped out and the front end started to wobble. What a thrill to speed down the road as my chubby cheeks flattened against my fat face.

Forty years later the same question popped into my mind while cruising on my motorcycle on I-75 out of Detroit. This time I rode my red-and-black Honda Valkyrie Interstate. This six-cylinder 1500cc beauty, designed for power and speed, glided down the interstate.

How fast will it go? I knew how to find out. Pulling back on the throttle, the bike surged from 60 to 70 to 80. A quick breath later my speedometer shouted 95.

BAM! My adult brain screamed, "Is this safe? Do you want to get hurt like your friend who wrecked his cycle? What will happen to your body when it hits the pavement at this speed?" I backed off. I played it safe. Even as I write, I regret never finding out what it was like to go full throttle on my red-and-black beast.

Looking back on your life, can you identify with this story? In younger days you took calculated risks. You rolled the dice. You wanted to see how fast it would go. But as you matured, you backed off. The adult in you insisted on playing it safe.

As years turned into decades, playing it safe seemed wise. Why take unnecessary risks? I convinced myself only fools lived at full throttle speed. My life operated around questions like these:

- What if the move to the neighboring state doesn't improve my life?
- What if my ideas are ridiculed?
- What if the job change turns into a train wreck?

- What if the boss says, "No"?
- What if no one reads what I write?

That kind of thinking made me cautious. Small wonder I eased back on the throttle. The winds of full throttle living no longer rushed past my cheeks. I traded it for a slow coast down a long hill. No wonder life slid into a predictable and safe ride.

Then, I did the unthinkable.

I walked away from a career of 30 years in which I had invested everything. It was the only world I had known all those years. For the next 12 months, no one gave me a weekly paycheck.

As you might imagine, life is no longer predictable. Instead, it is an exhilarating challenge. The wind of full throttle living once again blows through my hair as I reinvent myself.

This isn't a campaign for you to quit your job. You might, however, be able to tweak your present life situation to start living a full life. But you might need to move on. Maybe you even need to make a drastic change.

Apply this to your life:

1. Am I really living life to the fullest right now?

2. If not, what is keeping me from living a full life?

3. What changes do I need to make so I can live life full throttle?

# CHAPTER 3: CONQUER YOUR BUCKET LIST

Do you have a bucket list? More people than ever have one, thanks largely to the release of the movie by that title. Let me state the painfully obvious: To conquer your bucket list, you must first have one! If your bucket list of unfulfilled dreams is empty, you need to start dreaming again.

C. S. Lewis once said, "You are never too old to set a new goal or dream a new dream." Regardless of your age, you ought to have a list of dreams you are working to fulfill. If your bucket is empty spend some time with an eight-year-old and talk to them about their dreams. Conduct an interview. Ask them about their plans in the future. Listen closely and before long your bucket will start to fill up!

What skill have you always wanted to acquire but never did? Is there a country you have wanted to visit for years but just never got to? Why haven't you finished that college degree or taken that art class or written that book? How long do you plan to put off that fishing trip to the remote part of Canada? Dream and dream big. Fill up that bucket.

And who said you need to put your dreams in a bucket? If it is a rule that dreams must go in a bucket then break the rule. Any time I've ever stored something in a bucket, it started to rot or rust. Dreams are too precious to allow them to rot or rust.

Maybe we really ought to be talking about our crockpot list. At one point in time every kitchen in America had a crockpot. They were so handy. All you had to do was throw some meat and other stuff inside, put a lid on it, turn it on, and in five hours it was time to eat. The crockpot slowly cooked what was inside to perfection. Things never rot in a crockpot.

To conquer your bucket list, you ought to consider moving its items from the bucket to the crockpot. Let your dreams slow cook in your mind instead of rot or rust in the bucket. Pick one dream to start working on. What will it take to make it a reality? How much will it cost? How much time will it take? Run those questions through your mind until the ingredients start to come together. Before long it will be time to take it out of the crockpot and enjoy it.

Consider starting a notebook for your crockpot list. On each page, write one item from your list at the top. Write down all your thoughts about that item. For example, if you are at work and you have an interesting thought from your list, capture it by writing it on the page reserved for that item. Maybe you will think of a way to accomplish that item inexpensively or of a resource to check or of a friend to invite as a participant. Write it down. Allow each page in your notebook to simmer in your mind. But do not let it overcook! When the time comes to jump out of that plane or take that art class, do it!

Apply this to your life:

1. If you haven't written out a crockpot list, do it now. List 10 things you want to do before you die.

2. Prioritize the list.

3. Next to the top three items, place a date by which you will have accomplished these high priority items.

4. Revisit the list every six months to update it.

# CHAPTER 4: TRY A LOT OF STUFF, KEEP WHAT WORKS

In seventh grade a student gave a speech on how to shave. He announced 99% of first-time shaving strokes take place at the precise same spot. Why? A habit drives us. It feels right. It is comfortable to make the first swipe under the left sideburn. So, again and again, that's what we do. But if there is a better way to shave we will never discover it.

We have placed comfort over trying to find the best way.

Try this mini-experiment. Interlace your fingers by clasping your hands together. Is your left or right thumb on top? Now, dare to do it just the opposite. Place the other thumb in the top position. Feels uncomfortable, doesn't it? We tend to do the same things over and over because we are comfortable with how we do them, not because it is the best way.

We usually don't like to try new stuff. Why? We have become comfortable doing things the same way. Repetition is comforting. Who wants to do something differently if the way we do it feels so right?

But what if by maintaining the same way, you miss out on the best way?

Trying a lot of stuff means we must be willing to leave the comfort zone behind. And the way to do that is to imagine the reward. Think of the men who moved to California to set up mining camps in the 19th century. How could they leave the comforts of home and family to live in a tent and dig rocks? They went because they were driven with the thought of a huge reward: gold.

What if by maintaining the same way, you miss the best way?

You start your day the same way. You have a morning routine. Why not start the morning differently and see what happens? Maybe instead of starting your day on Facebook you should review your to-do list. Try praying before you run out the door. Read something inspiring prior to the craziness of the day. On the way to work, grab a Chai tea instead of a coffee.

What if by maintaining the same way, you miss the best way?

Think of your job. What do you do every day without even thinking to accomplish a task? Identify the critical routine tasks and try a different approach. Experiment. You might discover there is a far more productive way to succeed. If you are a salesperson, try making calls by the referral system. If you deliver mail, try a different route. If you are a preacher, write a sermon with two points instead of three. If you are a teacher stand in a different spot to lecture. Is there a better way?

What if by maintaining the same way, you miss the best way?

What about how you handle those difficult moments with your teenage son or daughter? Yelling at them is your immediate and most-used method of discipline. But what if there is a better way? Try different things and see what happens. Reward them. Befriend them. Try a lot of stuff and see what works.

Through the experimentation process toss what does not work. The effort was not wasted. You discovered an ineffective way to do it.

Dare to do things in ways that stretch your comfort zone. Keep trying. When you hit upon a better way it will be an exciting moment.

If you always do what you have always done, you will always miss the best way to get something done.

Try a lot of stuff and see what works.

Apply this to your life:

1. What are you going to try to do differently?

2. What have you been doing the same way for a long time that you might be able to do a better way?

3. The next time you drive to work, go a different way. How did it feel?

4. Why is it so uncomfortable to do things a different way?

# CHAPTER 5: ALL LIFE IS AN EXPERIMENT

When I lived in Monroe, Michigan, Panera Bread topped the list of my favorite places to eat. On each visit, I ordered the same thing: A Fuji apple chicken salad with a chicken Frontega panini. My wife would make fun of me for ordering the same thing. Why did I do it? I was afraid that, by making a different decision, I would end up with something I didn't like.

I forgot that all of life is an experiment. We can say this because the results of our decisions are unknown. Choose one action and we get a particular result. Choose a different action and the results change.

When faced with a decision we tend to stick with the tried and true based on past experiences. I do this with food (see above), vacations (I've been to Guatemala four times), and the kind of cars I buy (cheap and ugly).

Here's the problem. When you fail to see life as an experiment, you miss out on new discoveries. Think of all the great scientific discoveries. Some were made by accident. But most of them happened because of a scientific experiment. A scientist came up with a working hypothesis. He or she tested the hypothesis. Results were analyzed and conclusions drawn.

This process sounds tedious, but think of the results. You are reading this on a computer. The computer is the compilation of thousands of past experiments. Experimentation bursts through the darkness and illuminates the present. We are propelled forward in a positive way.

When we fail to experiment, we fail to make significant life-changing discoveries.

Are you like me, wanting to cling to the familiar and not experiment? Here are four ways to start experimenting so you can discover a better life.

1. Remind yourself that most decisions do not result in permanent changes. There is no need to be paralyzed for fear of making a bad decision. If you make a bad decision in an effort to try something different, so what? The sun really will come up tomorrow.

2. You will not always make perfect decisions. That's okay. Stop beating yourself up when one of your decisions ends badly. The secret in making your life an experiment is to embrace your bad decisions. Here's why: Your bad decisions form the curriculum you must study to improve your life. The choices you make give you the knowledge you need to increase quality living.

3. When your decisions bring poor results, make the commitment to stop saying, "Oh well." This is your opportunity to analyze what happened. You now have raw data to examine. Ask yourself why the results were poor. What went wrong? How can you improve next time? What is the biggest lesson you can learn from the failed decision?

4. Take the lessons learned and keep experimenting. Historians disagree on the exact number of failures Thomas Edison endured while perfecting the light bulb. But many agree he experimented with more than a thousand different filaments before getting it right. His attitude is the kind of attitude I want. He said that each failure was not a failure but a success, because he learned that filament type would not work.

Here's a new paradigm to consider: Think, explore, decide, learn. Experiment. Don't quit. Refuse to let failure stop you. Try different things.

You are on the verge of discovering life-changing truths when you become an experimenter.

Apply this to your life:

1. What is your first experiment?

2. Plan on how to conduct your experiment. What will be different? How will you do it?

3. Pick a date and get started.

4. Evaluate at the end of the experiment.

# CHAPTER 6: LIVE LIFE INTENSELY CURIOUS

On August 6, 2012, a United States NASA rover landed on Mars. It flew 350 billion miles and landed one and a half miles from the targeted landing site. Aboard the rover, along with a plaque bearing the signatures of President Barack Obama and Vice President Joe Biden, was an autograph of 12-year-old Clara Ma from Kansas. Who is she? Why was her autograph on the Mars rover?

From 2009-2011 the public could participate in a contest to name the rover. More than 1.2 million people submitted names. Clara's autograph is on the rover because NASA selected her suggested name. Do you remember the name of the rover? Curiosity. She said, "Curiosity is the passion that drives us through our everyday lives." Curiosity made it to Mars.

It isn't surprising the winning name came from a 12-year-old. Think of how kids learn. They ask lots of questions. They look at their world with curious eyes.

- "Why is the sky blue?"
- "Where did I come from?"
- "Why does water run downhill?"
- "How does grass grow?"

And as they ask questions they learn about their world and life.

Years ago I substitute taught seventh graders. They had to review a vocabulary list. Seized by a moment of inspiration I decided to teach them the most important word they would ever learn: "why." I told them "why" would unlock the mysteries of life; the world would open up. As I talked, a few students got it. They started shouting out "Why?" after each sentence. I told them to practice on their teachers the rest of the day. Their assignment was to ask their teachers "why?" through the rest of their classes. I'm pretty sure, by the end of the day, the teachers hated the substitute from the second period English class.

Here's the problem. As we age, we tend to forget we learn best by being intensely curious. The giants of the past never lost their curiosity.

While writing this chapter, I traveled to the Phoenix Art Museum to see a special Leonardo da Vinci exhibit. On display was his Codex Leicester. This book of scientific inquiry consists of 72 pages. Bill Gates purchased it from Armand Hammer in 1984 for $30,802,500. It is the most valuable book in the world.

The book contained scientific observations sprinkled with occasional sketches. In the middle of these observations was an unusual looking symbol. The interpretive display revealed that the symbol simply meant: "Why is this?"

According to the book *How to Think Like da Vinci* by Michael Gelb, one of the defining hallmarks of da Vinci's life was his curiosity. Asking "why" to his observations yielded amazing discoveries. Why do birds fly? Why do river banks erode? Why is the body perfectly symmetrical?

His curiosity forced him to search for answers to the "why" questions. People gasp while reading da Vinci's notebooks because they see sketches for things that would not be manufactured for another 450 years. How could he possibly have a sketch of a helicopter which wouldn't be invented for centuries? It all hinged on his curiosity.

Are you living life intensely curious?

Apply this to your life:

Try this experiment for 24 hours: Force yourself to be intensely curious. Pay attention to what's going on around you and inside you. Make a list of the questions resulting from your curiosity. Your list might look like this:

1. Why did I snap at my friend when they corrected me?

2. Why did my spouse not respond to me when I asked about their day?

3. Why does my kid ignore me in the morning?

4. Why do I want to run someone off the road after they cut me off?

Keep a list of questions like these. The next day, review them and see what you can learn. I'm certain you will learn at least one important life-changing truth.

Why do I sometimes not want to be
with Teresa?
why do I worry so much about
Luke & Angie

# CHAPTER 7: JOY IS PROPORTIONATE TO YOUR LEVEL OF GRATITUDE

My junior year in high school, I worked at the Coca-Cola Bottling Company in Goshen, Indiana. The workers on my shift included Roger. Yes, THAT Roger. THE same Roger who made girls swoon with his rugged good looks, curly hair, and devilish smile. And yes, the same Roger who proudly drove the new 1972 Z28 Camaro his daddy gave him. If I was sure of anything, I was sure I wanted to be Roger.

But Roger had one outstanding flaw. He radiated unhappiness. He wore a grin on his face, but a dark cloud followed his every step.

Ever notice how unhappy some successful people seem to be? By all outward appearances they have it all: money, big house, power, and a new convertible parked in the driveway. They should be filled with joy. But too many times it's the opposite. Why? What is the problem? Here's the answer: Too often they focus on what they DON'T have, instead of focusing on what they DO have.

What about you? Is there real joy in your life? This lesson from *Tom's List* reminds us joy is NOT in proportion to the amount of good stuff in your life. Nope. The amount of joy in your life is in proportion to your level of gratitude. Little gratitude equals little joy. Much gratitude equals much joy.

On the morning of my sixtieth birthday I awoke at 2:20 realizing my life had entered a new decade. As I thought of my life, I realized many of my major goals remained unmet. My mind wandered to the lack of quality material things in my life.

My only car was old. My limited cable TV didn't carry the *Monday Night Football* channel. The house I recently moved into was small.

On the opening day of my next decade, I headed down the dreary road of self-pity.

It was on that day I made the decision to write about *Tom's List*. When I opened the folded piece of paper containing the list my eyes landed on commandment number 7: "Joy is proportionate to your level of gratitude." Bang! I began to think of reasons to be thankful.

Sure, my old car had 150,000 miles on it, but I had no car payment! I still missed *Monday Night Football*, but I realized my recent move allowed me to see more Chicago Bears football than before my move. And just maybe this smaller house would be paid off in my lifetime.

One by one, the good things in my life paraded through my mind. It was like watching a parade of goodness march across my field of vision. Good health, wonderful wife, terrific kids and grandkids all strolled past and smiled. Their smiles were infectious. Before long I put on the brakes and exited Self-Pity Road.

Thinking about all the good things in my life had greater impact than taking some sort of magical happy pill. Life seemed different. The day became brighter. I didn't feel quite as old. The angels sang the Hallelujah Chorus.

You may be going through difficulties and headed down the road of self-pity, but hit the brakes! Think about the good things in your life. Did you wake up this morning? Did you sleep in a warm bed last night? Did you have toothpaste to smear on that toothbrush? Close your eyes and let the parade of goodness strut across the screen of your mind.

Let the parade begin. Watch your level of joy increase.

Apply this to your life:

1. Make a list of the top 10 things for which you are thankful.

2. Remind yourself that many people do not have a list like yours.

3. Be glad for what you have!

# CHAPTER 8: WHEN YOU GET INSPIRED, LEVERAGE IT TO THE HILT

In May 2014, in Petersburg, Virginia, firefighters responded to an emergency call. First responders pulled a woman and her dog Kaiser, a German Shepherd mix, from the burning house. A quick assessment revealed Kaiser was in far worse condition than the owner. Firefighter Josh Moore did something he had never done before. He strapped an oxygen mask onto Kaiser's face. In a few minutes the tail of the unresponsive dog started to twitch. After a three-day stay at the vet, an inspired Kaiser went home.

What happened? Kaiser became "inspired." When we think of that word, we forget the archaic meaning is "to breathe life" back into something. Like a dog. Like a depressed person. Like someone who is "uninspired."

Whatever the source of inspiration, when it comes, leverage it to the hilt.

Too often we are so busy that the moments of inspiration almost go unnoticed. Have you ever been at work and had a brilliant flash of an idea streak across your mind, only to have it vaporize into oblivion? What was the idea? You can't remember. You were too busy to capture it and now it's gone. Mark it down as an opportunity missed.

When those moments of inspiration come, grab them. Write them down. Stop what you are doing and send yourself an email with the idea as the subject. Grab a pen and write on the palm of your hand if needed. DON'T let that inspired thought get away. It might be one that will change your life.

At the appropriate time, analyze what you have captured. What does it mean? Why did it fly across the consciousness of your mind? What would happen if you would act upon that inspired thought? Why did the thought stir you on the inside?

Some inspired thoughts will turn out to be only disappointing distractions. But many of them can be leveraged to your benefit. When you've decided the thought is worthy of attention, don't let it sit there. Do something with it.

- Is this an idea to be studied in greater detail?
- Is there a task to be scheduled?
- Do you need to explore a career change?
- Should you ask your friend to forgive you?

Did you know that a beautiful shot of espresso starts to lose its flavor in a matter of minutes? Like a perfect shot of espresso, your inspired thought is fragile. The longer it sits on the shelf of your mind the more power it loses. Don't waste it.

I decided to write a book. What an inspiring moment! My life lit up just thinking about it. But that was 25 years ago. And, you guessed it, no book. I failed to leverage my inspired moment. Don't make the same mistake.

What inspired thought waltzes across the dance floor of your mind? Capture it and share it with other readers. You might inspire someone else.

Apply this to your life:

1. Decide what method you will use to capture your moments of inspiration. Will it be a simple notepad? Or will you use Evernote on your iPhone?

2. Make sure your capturing device is always close to you.

3. Every morning, take some time to process your captured items.

4. Follow through on the list.

# CHAPTER 9: HAVE A STRONG BIAS TOWARD ACTION; BE KNOWN AS A PERSON OF ACTION

How would you define "filibuster"? Here's my definition: "Stupidity expressed by a never-ending torrent of words." Filibuster and I first crossed paths in junior high. My civics teacher explained it as a tactic employed in Congress to delay or kill the passage of a proposed bill. A politician simply stood up and talked endlessly until there remained no time to debate the bill, killing it by words.

We can trace the origination of the word back to the Dutch, where it meant "pirate." Makes sense. When a concept for making positive change dies by being talked to death in a sea of words we are robbed of the potential good. And the one who does all the big talking is the pirate.

Are you a pirate? We are quick to point fingers at politicians for talking good ideas into an early grave, but what about you? Do you rob yourself of treasure chests filled with promising ideas because you talk them to death? Are you filibustering your great ideas into a watery grave of words? Are they sinking into oblivion before even seeing the light of day?

When you talk and never do, you are robbing yourself and others of a potential good.

The *Tom's List* commandment for this week reminds us it is far better to be known as a person of action than a person of words.

     - Why do we talk our ideas to death?
     - It feels safer to talk instead of act.
     - Talking means putting little skin in the game.
     - Some people like to hear themselves babble.
     - When we keep talking, it feels like we are making progress.

But there comes a time when we must shut up and do it. Mr. T, the great thinker from the old TV show "The A-Team," often said: "Shut up, fool!" And the fool is you. Stop being a fool by thinking words without action will get the job done. Yes, we need words and discussion. But when the time comes to act, shut up and go do it.

And if you refuse this advice? You will go to your grave with a head filled with dead ideas because you failed to act.

- You will never get published.
- You will never see Italy.
- You will never start that business.
- You will never obtain that degree.
- You will never stand on the mountain top.
- You will never be reconciled with your son or daughter.
- You will never run your marathon.

All you did was talk about it. Proud of yourself? Wasn't it fun? You played it safe. It cost you nothing. Listening to yourself babble became a form of entertainment. You talked a great talk, but you failed to do.

Stop being a foolish pirate. Stop talking. Shut up. Go and do it.

Apply this to your life:

1. Listen and watch yourself for the next 24 hours to determine if you are a doer or a talker.

2. What do you need to stop talking about and start doing?

3. Make the commitment to start on it immediately.

# CHAPTER 10: FOCUS: 20% OF YOUR INPUTS DRIVE 80% OF YOUR OUTPUTS

Vilfredo Pareto was an Italian thinker who specialized in connecting dots. Could you connect the dots between the number of peas in a pod with land distribution? Pareto did. He observed 20% of the pea pods in his garden contained 80% of the total pea crop. Then, studying the distribution of land in Italy, he realized 20% of the people owned 80% of the land. The ratio 80:20 struck a chord.

Pareto investigated and discovered the ratio held true in many areas of life. He concluded 20% of effort brings 80% of the results. Let's say it in even simpler terms. The majority of what happens in life is from a small number of causes.

Here are several examples:

    - 20% of the congregation makes 80% of the complaints.
    - 20% of your friends create 80% of your relational happiness.
    - 20% of your possessions are used 80% of the time.
    - 20% of your posts generates 80% of your blog traffic.
    - 20% of the sales force makes 80% of the company's sales.
    - 20% of what you read impacts 80% of your life.
    - 20% of your diet contains 80% of the calories.

These observations may appear to be an oddity to amuse the curious. But wait. Stop and think about how the Pareto Principle applies to you. This could be life changing.

There are two simple steps to make the magic happen.

First, answer this question: "What activities in my life produce the best results?" Do you find yourself renewed by walking through the woods? Does 20 minutes on the treadmill energize you? When you read a motivational book are you ready to tackle the world? When you read the Bible in the morning, does it help you throughout the day? What is it that puts you in a good mood?

Second, do more of the things on your list from your answer to the first question. Why do we spend so much time doing unproductive things?

Maybe it's a habit. Maybe you've never thought about it. Maybe you are on autopilot as you go through the day. But your life can be more productive and happier if you make the decision to focus more on the things that make a difference. Decide now to focus your energy and attention on activities that produce the greatest results.

Don't be legalistic about the principle. It doesn't apply to every situation. Sometimes the percentage fluctuates. Instead of 80:20 the ratio might be 70:30. Don't worry about that. But focus on doing more of what matters. And the opposite rings true: Stop wasting so much time on activities that produce little results.

Apply this to your life:

1. What time waster are you going to throttle?

2. What are you going to do more of that produces big results for you?

3. What is the most important lesson you've learned from the Pareto Principle?

# CHAPTER 11: PRIORITIZATION: FOCUS ON THE THINGS THAT MATTER MOST

At the age of nine, I made a discovery that brought more joy than opening a box of Lucky Charms and discovering the box only contained flavored marshmallows. I discovered the power of focus.

The discovery came when my brother and I got our hands on a magnifying glass. The eyes of a grasshopper transformed into an image of monster movie proportions while under a magnifying glass. We were not allowed to play with matches, but with our new toy, who needed matches? We could burn holes right through baseball cards and make dead leaves turn into smoke signals.

At an early age, I learned the power of focus brings clarity and intensity into your life.

To harness the power of clarity, you must get the right perspective. To clearly see the fascinating eyes of a grasshopper, the magnifying glass needed to be focused just right. This meant moving the glass closer and farther out until the image became sharp. Details could be gained only when achieving the right perspective.

You gain tremendous power in life when you get the right perspective. To get the right perspective, you need to focus. Change your view slightly. Pull back and see what happens. Then lean in closer and take another look. Find the sweet spot so you can see the issues in your life with clarity.

Intensity is the other powerful byproduct of focus. Do you lack intensity? Are you just going through life on cruise control? Focus is the answer.

Focus is the reason the magnifying glass can burn holes through cardboard and start fires. It takes the energy from the sun and, when the right focus is achieved, places all the energy into one tiny hot spot.

This is a challenge in my life. My iPhone constantly fragments my thinking. Alarms go off and a ping here, and a ding-dong there distract me from the task I am attempting to achieve. I can't resist checking my phone to see who is now following me on Twitter. I'm certain the urgent beep signaling the arrival of a new email will change my life. Who can possibly focus?

But if we are to focus so we can gain intensity, distractions must go. Turn your phone off while concentrating. And do you really need the voice of Judge Judy in the background while trying to focus? When you get rid of the distractions, you will gain intensity.

Now comes the wisdom of *Tom's List*. Take the power of focus and apply it to the important areas of your life. Prioritize where to place your focus. Focus is good when you are trying to watch TV, but it is life changing when you are putting together a to-do list for the week or working on your life goals. Learn to focus on the important issues in your life.

So where are you going to aim your magnifying glass?

Apply this to your life:

1. In what area of your life do you need to focus the most?

2. For one week, take 15 minutes every day to focus on what is most important.

3. Keep a journal and track your thoughts and progress.

# CHAPTER 12: WORK ONLY ON THINGS THAT WILL MAKE A GREAT DEAL OF DIFFERENCE IF YOU SUCCEED

Guess what? I just completed level 20,000 of Smash a Zit!

Are you annoyed when you see posts like this on Facebook? Who really cares? It's a measure of proficiency which ranks you relative to other players. But I'm no longer annoyed when I see these posts. They make me sad.

Why? I think of the time and effort spent on earning "badges" for a meaningless game. If these energies were redirected, a lot of good could be accomplished.

I'm not against playing games or relaxing. Time spent doing these things initiates a restorative process to the soul. But there is a bigger, more pressing truth to examine.

Great care must be given to assure we spend the bulk of our time and energy on things that really make a difference when we succeed. What a waste to work hard, find success, and then discover it made no lasting contribution to your life or to others.

Consider this list of accomplishments:

 - Watched the entire *West Wing* TV series.
 - Learned to complete a Rubik's cube in less than five minutes.
 - Trained yourself to ride a unicycle.
 - Memorized the names of every character in the *Lord of the Rings* trilogy.

These are all cool. When you complete one of these tasks you feel a measure of pride. Go ahead, pat yourself on the back. Now look at this list:

 - Teach yourself to be conversant in Spanish.
 - Learn how to bind a book.
 - Start a website to inspire readers as you share your thoughts.
 - Read the top ten greatest books of all time.

The items on this list are also cool. You can feel pride at the completion of any item on the list. But do you see the difference? These goals make a difference. Your investment of time and energy pay off far beyond making yourself feel good or entertained. Completing one of these goals might make a real difference in your life or someone else's. Success makes a real positive impact.

Here's the defining question: When I complete my goal, my job, my task, what will I have accomplished? Be ruthless. Strive for clarity. And the follow-up question screaming to be answered is this: Will it make any difference?

It will be time well spent to examine your goals. Be brave and even examine how you make a living. When it's all over, will you have made a difference?

One of my heroes is my brother Terry. He worked for many years in a factory. The job paid well. But at the end of the day it was just a way to pay the bills. He decided to get a degree and pursue a more meaningful career. While working full time, he enrolled in a school more than 50 miles from his house and obtained a degree in engineering. Now, for many years, he has poured his life into a job with meaning. He works for a company that designs and makes replacement body parts. If you have an artificial anything in your body, you might owe my brother a note of gratitude.

Learn to work on things that make a difference if you succeed.

Apply this to your life:

1. Make a list of the five things you need to change.

2. Dare to ask yourself the hard question. At the end of the day, will those changes make a genuine difference?

3. If the answer is "no" to the above question, discard it and focus on the other changes.

# CHAPTER 13: THE BEST WAY TO PREDICT THE FUTURE IS TO CREATE IT

In the classic movie *Back to the Future*, Marty McFly goes back in time and accidentally destroys his present reality. How? His mother-to-be falls for him. To correct this turn of events he must go back to the past to create the kind of future he knows and wants.

When most people talk about the future they dream of what it will be like. They think about their life in five, ten, or 15 years. This kind of future dreaming assumes we are passive recipients of whatever happens. True, in some ways we are helpless about the days and years to come. We have no control over the weather, government, or the actions of most people.

There is, however, a real sense in which we can control the future. The key to controlling the future is to control ourselves. When we do that, the ability to create the future is not far away.

When we control ourselves we can start to plan for the kind of future we want. In Stephen Covey's classic *7 Habits of Highly Effective People* he urges readers to start with the end in mind. When creating your own future there is no better advice to be found.

What kind of future do you want? Start dreaming about how you want life to look five, ten, or 15 years from now. Once you get a dream in your mind, embrace it, then work to make it a reality. If you follow this simple advice, you can create your own future.

For many years I never gave thought to retirement. Retirement was a long way off. My plan involved worrying about it later. But the day came when I realized the noise in the back of my mind was retirement knocking at the door. I had a "come to Jesus" talk with myself.

Given my then-current reality, retirement looked grim. Financially, I had not prepared. My monthly pension would pay only for groceries. Now what? I began to dream about the kind of retirement I wanted. From that dreamy moment to this moment I've been working to be ready for retirement.

I dreamed.
I embraced the dream.
I started working toward the dream.
I am creating my own future.

Of all the items on *Tom's List* to this point, I view this one as the most powerful. You do NOT need to be a passive recipient of the future. You are not a victim of your circumstances.

What about you? What do you want your future to look like? Start dreaming now about the future. Begin with the end in mind. And once you have a clear picture of the future you want, then go out and create it. Dream. Plan. Work. Enjoy. Create your own future!

Apply this to your life:

1. Start dreaming of the kind of future you want.

2. Break the dream down into small steps.

3. Turn the steps into goals.

4. Watch your future unfold.

# CHAPTER 14: WORK HARDER ON YOURSELF THAN YOU DO ON YOUR JOB

You would never think your job might be your worst enemy. And I'm talking about a good-paying job. A job with great benefits. A job others might kill to get: Yes, THAT job. YOUR job might be the one thing keeping you from the life you were meant to live.

You work hard. You've become heavily invested in your job.

Arriving early in the morning, you give it all you've got until you crawl in bed at night.

The boss gives you a challenge and you spare no sacrifice to meet it.

Deadlines show up on your calendar and with superhuman effort you meet them.

You need additional training and so, with book in hand, you spend your evenings reading and studying.

With your success at work, you get more and more responsibility and a new title.

But the time will come when you say goodbye to your job. What then? What about you? What will happen to a good employee like you who has poured everything into the job, but ignored yourself?

There is great danger with any job, even a good job. The danger is you've focused on being a success at work but ignored being a success with yourself.

Don't confuse the two. You are more important than the work you do. You are more important than your employer. You are more important than the company's profit margin.

While pouring your life into your job, begin to think about pouring yourself into yourself. What would it look like if you started to spend more effort on succeeding in life than succeeding at work?

Start small. Begin by thinking of the vital areas of your life. Make a list. The list might include family, health, dreams, education, and God. Then ask a simple question: "What can I do to enrich my life in each area?"

What book can I read to become a better parent?

Is there a workout routine which, if followed, will extend the length and quality of my life?

What can I do to start realizing the dream which I shoved over in the corner when I got busy with my job?

How can I complete my education?

Is there one thing I can start doing each day to move God into the center of my life?

If all you do with your life is work for the man, pay bills, get a few promotions, and then sit around waiting for Mr. Grim Reaper to come knocking, you've settled for too little.

This is YOUR life. Don't let your job, as good as it might be, suck you dry. On purpose, start investing in yourself.

Trust me. You are worth it.

Apply this to your life:

1. Decide that you are important enough to invest in yourself. Be willing to make the investment.

2. Determine the one thing you're going to do to start investing in yourself.

# CHAPTER 15: YOU ARE THE SAME TODAY AS YOU WILL BE IN FIVE YEARS EXCEPT FOR THE PEOPLE YOU MEET AND THE BOOKS YOU READ

*Hyberbole: hy·per·bo·le; hī'pərbəlē; noun*
*exaggerated statements or claims not meant to be taken literally.*

Use hyperbole to make sure your point gets attention. This commandment from *Tom's List* is a master example. Is it true that "You are the same today as you will be in five years except for the people you meet and the books you read"? Yes, but the addition of the word "except" is an exaggeration to get your attention.

Here's the point: What you read and who you meet over an extended period of time results in a major transformational impact. With exposure to the sun as the day grows old, a rock becomes warm, even hot. As we read books and rub shoulders with people, we tend to take on the characteristics of what we've exposed ourselves to.

What we put in us, who we associate with, transforms us.

The real lesson is clear: Choose your books and friends with care. Exposure to them can change you for the better or the worse. If you read junk, it will drag you down. If you surround yourself with friends who are negative, you will become like them. Do yourself a favor and run with the winners, not the losers.

Think of the last three books you've read. What messages do they contain? If you start to take on the characteristics of what you've been reading, will the results be good or bad? I challenge you to make a list of three books that could add value to your life. Start reading those books. Expose yourself to books that build you up.

Do the same with your friends. Think of your closest friends. Are they making you more positive or more negative? When you get together, do you talk people down or talk them up? Do you talk about what's wrong with the church or what's right with the church? Think of the most positive and cheerful person you know. Take them out for coffee. Talk. Listen. Enjoy. Grow.

Does this really work? The best example I can give is my friendship with Tom Drake, who put this list together. We first met back in 1972. Having him in my life made me a better person. Across the years we touched base only once or twice a year. But with a wry grin on his face he encouraged me to read good books and be a good person.

Do you want to improve your life? Do you want to grow? Choose your books and friends with care.

Apply this to your life:

1. What book do you need to read? Make a list of the top ten books that could change your life. Check out the bestsellers list on Amazon for suggestions. Prioritize the list and start with No. 1.

2. Who do you need to have coffee with? Who is the one person you could learn the most from? Call them and schedule a meeting.

# CHAPTER 16: TAKE ADVANTAGE OF EVERY SPEAKING OPPORTUNITY AND OVER-PREPARE FOR IT

The goal of *Tom's List* is to stretch you to get more out of life. But I'm guessing most readers will break, not stretch, when they see the phrase "speaking opportunity." Getting up in front of a crowd is a terrifying idea to most people.

Maybe this words from Jerry Seinfeld captures your emotions when it comes to public speaking:

"According to most studies, people's number one fear is public speaking. Number two is death. Death is number two. Does that seem right? That means to the average person, if you have to go to a funeral, you're better off in the casket than doing the eulogy."

Thirty years ago I embarked on a career path that required me to speak in front of a group three to four times every week. Trust me, like everyone else, public speaking appeared on my "most afraid of this" list. But over time, it got easy. Now, when I speak, my biggest problem is waiting for my turn on the agenda.

Think of what you might miss if you fail to deal with this fear. You might refuse a promotion because it requires public speaking. Have you ever been asked to make a speech at a wedding, family gathering, or even a funeral but you had to refuse? Did you ever decide to take an adult ed class but bailed when you found it required standing up in front of the class to give a report?

When you get the opportunity to speak, never turn it down because you never know what doors it will open.

Maybe you will never get to the point where you thrill at the thought of speaking to a group. But here are a few tips to get you started. You can do this!

1. Over-prepare. Become an expert on the subject of your speech. Know your material better than Starbucks knows coffee. Go over your material

in front of a mirror. Challenge yourself to look more at your reflection than your notes as you practice.

2. Realize no one in the room knows exactly what you are going to say. You can deviate from your notes and get off script but no one will know it if you keep on going.

3. Forget about the people looking at you and focus on the message you are sharing. The surefire method to crash and burn during a speech is to start asking yourself, "I wonder what those people are thinking about me? Am I looking stupid?" Focus on the message far more than the people.

You can overcome your fear and speak in public. And if you try it, you might find you like it.

Apply this to your life:

1. When was the last time you had the opportunity to speak? How did it go?

2. Decide the next time you get an invitation to speak, you will do it.

3. Prepare carefully and plan on success.

# CHAPTER 17: BELIEVE THAT YOUR SELF-MADE HABITS WILL DETERMINE YOUR FUTURE SUCCESS

Tony Dungy was the only NFL coach to reach the playoffs in ten consecutive years. He achieved success on a unique coaching philosophy based on the power of habits. Dungy believed in the fierce combative action on the field: a player reacts in split seconds according to established habits.

Habits fascinate me. When a habit kicks in, it is as if the brain goes on auto-pilot. The habits we've created are always in the background ready to run the show if needed.

Years ago, while driving a long distance at night, I fought to stay awake. I grabbed the wheel harder, determined to make my destination. The next thing I knew, the car sat on the side of the road as I snapped back to reality from behind the wheel. Shaking my head, I realized I had no memory of the last 50 miles of the trip. What happened? I must have fallen asleep. But I am confident of this: the power of habit came to my rescue and guided the car safely to the curb.

Habits are always there, guiding, directing, taking over when we don't even know it.

Here's a critical truth about habits: they can guide you to success or drive you to failure. Start observing your habits. Ask yourself if they help or hurt you. Isolate the ones that steer you toward failure.

You would think the next step would be to stamp out a bad habit. But that's not going to happen. You cannot make a bad habit disappear. But here's what you can do: You can change it.

This is what Tony Dungy believed as he built championship football teams. He decided the way to take players to the next level was to isolate their bad habits and change them into good habits.

Tony believed habits were made up of a three-step loop: cue, routine, reward. The cue is a trigger which awakens a habit. The routine is the action phase. When the action is completed a reward is received. Here's the trick to changing a bad habit: Keep the cue and the reward but change the routine. Dungy knew a player could change a bad habit if the start and finish looked the same and only the routine changed.

The refrigerator door opens (cue), you grab a piece of pie and eat it (routine), and you are rewarded with a fuller stomach. That's a bad habit. Using Tony's method for changing bad habits alters the routine. The refrigerator door opens (cue), you grab a piece of fruit and eat it (routine), and you are rewarded with a fuller stomach. Change the routine but keep the cue and reward.

Now you know the secret to dealing with bad habits leading to failure instead of success. Change them into positive habits.

Success or failure rests upon habits. Make sure your habits are taking you down the right road.

Apply this to your life:

1. Make a list of bad habits that need to change.

2. Of those on your list, which one would change your life the most if it changed?

3. Analyze the habit you need to change with the three-step loop: cue, routine, reward.

4. Apply this three-step process to change your most destructive habit.

# CHAPTER 18: DON'T BELIEVE IN WORDS — ONLY BELIEVE IN BEHAVIORS

*"Actions speak louder than words, but not nearly as often." Mark Twain*

I'm a lover of words. Go ahead. Laugh. But I've discovered words contain the power to educate, amuse, and transform lives.

Not long ago, I substitute taught in a county juvenile detention center. My students for the day were teen criminals. Teaching a captive audience is interesting. One class in particular captured my attention. How do you lift the spirits of high school girls locked up and being forced to go to school? Why, teach them a new word!

I introduced them to one of my favorite words: salubrious. It's a fun word to pronounce that means "having a healthy benefit." They laughed and their eyes lit up. They got it.

But there's a problem. Words roll off our tongue like Google search returns on a laptop. Have you ever been trapped in a conversation with a "Talk Monster" who terrifies you by never taking a breath?

It's really frightening when words roll unexamined off our tongue because too often we say things we don't mean.

We stretch the truth: I can finish the project in one day.

We make promises we cannot keep: I will never disappoint you.

We lie: Don't worry, I know what needs to be done and I'll do it.

This is why we must never rely only on the words spoken. We must also factor in the behavior of the one speaking. Talk is cheap. It is fun. It is easy. But the only way to validate words is to examine behavior.

Sometimes it makes little difference if the words you hear are reliable. But when careless words impact me, it's a different story.

I've learned the hard way that those who tell me they have my back too often don't.

Experience has taught me that a promise isn't always a promise no matter how much they promise!

"You can count on me" doesn't always mean I can count on them.

And "let's be equal partners" might not mean we split the profits 50/50.

I'm going to give people the benefit of the doubt. But I've learned to watch and see if the words ring true with the corresponding behavior. That's not being sneaky. That's being smart. And I like to be smart.

Can you think of a time when the behavior did not match the words?

Apply this to your life:

1. The most important conversation taking place is the one in your head. For the next 24 hours, listen carefully to what's being said. Do you talk a good talk but lack the behavior to back it up? Work on matching your words with your behavior.

2. Watch and listen to the people around you. Do their actions match their words? If not, tread lightly when interacting with them.

# CHAPTER 19: COURAGE: RESOLVE TO DO ONE THING EVERY DAY THAT YOU FEAR; BUST OUT OF YOUR COMFORT ZONES

Have you ever decided you were sick of playing it safe? Have you ever been tempted to just take a leap into the unknown? But when it came time to leap, you backed down?

Several years ago, while in Guatemala, I decided for once in my life I would not play it safe. That decision led me to Finca Filadelfia outside of Antigua, a coffee plantation that has also gained fame for conducting zip line tours. The ride up the mountain in a Unimog Mercedes Benz transport vehicle put enough fear in me to call it a day. But I had determined to look fear in the eye and not blink.

Standing on the edge of a zip line platform epitomized all my fears. I'm not a fan of heights. I'm afraid of every ride at the amusement park. But there I stood, looking out across the canyon. It stretched 1,700 feet across and 500 above the valley floor. I had made the mistake of standing there and watching the armed guard leap off the platform with a disturbing whirring sound, getting smaller and smaller until he disappeared into the distance.

Now it was my turn. The guard used the walkie-talkie to verify they were ready for me on the other end. The guide on the platform next to me turned and said, "OK, your turn. Go!" I blinked. No way. I couldn't shove off. The canyon in front of me laughed as I shrunk back in fear. The guide told me to take my time, counted down and again commanded "Go!" I blinked again.

By the third time I decided to do it if it killed me, knowing it probably would. I jumped off the platform and raced across the canyon. The line screamed and I felt like doing the same. I made it. When I arrived on the other side, saturated in adrenaline, I asked when the truck would come and pick me up. The guard laughed. He took perverse pleasure in announcing the only way back was to strap on and go back the way I came.

Looking back, I realize the leap became a defining moment for me. It made me realize fear did not need to rule my life.

I know of only one way to come out of your comfort zone: Take a deep breath and jump. And when you do, you might discover it will improve your life.

What are some things in your life you refuse to do because of fear? Do you see any of those fears on the following list?

- Ask your boss for a raise.
- Go to the doctor to get those strange symptoms diagnosed.
- Proactively reach out to your kid who doesn't talk to you.
- Pay off your car loan.
- Ask your spouse to forgive you.
- Quit the job you hate and do work that fulfills you.

Jump! Leap! Why wouldn't you take action to improve your life? Oh, that's right: Fear. I get it.

Let me tell you what I've decided about fear. I love being afraid. Why? Fear sets the stage for courage. Without fear, there can be no courage.

I pity the person who announces he's afraid of nothing. He can never be courageous because there's no fear to overcome.

Are you a courageous person? Then you are no stranger to fear. Embrace the fear but don't stop there. Use your fear to step up and become a courageous person.

Make the decision to be courageous every day.

Apply this to your life:

1. Look at your life. What is it you fear? Make a list.

2. Now, review the list and write beside each fear things you can do that require courage.

3. Begin each morning this week picking one thing from the list you can do that day.

4. Say goodbye to your comfort zones.

# CHAPTER 20: SELF-DISCIPLINE IS THE NO. 1 DELINEATING FACTOR BETWEEN HIGH ACHIEVERS AND LOW ACHIEVERS

At the age of 42, I decided to learn how to play the piano. Why not? How hard could it be? For about six weeks I took lessons. Once in a while I even practiced. My piano teacher announced he was putting together a recital. He encouraged me to participate, suggesting I could be an inspiration to other adults who wanted to learn piano.

The big day came. I sat on the front row with the other students. The next oldest recitalist had been on planet Earth about ten years. The student before me, at nine years of age, walked with confidence to the piano bench. He sat down and played like Sergei Rachmaninoff. As I went to the piano my confidence level limped along beside me. I sat down, started to play, and had to stop and restart three times. At last I made it to the end of my rendition of "Blue Butterfly."

What made the difference? Was the nine-year-old smarter than I? Doubtful. Were his fingers longer and more able to stretch across the keyboard? Nope. Here's the difference: He had more self-discipline than I, which enabled him to practice more.

When you look at successful people, do you find yourself wondering how they managed to be so lucky? You tell yourself they seem to always get the big breaks. Why, you wonder to yourself, can't I ever get lucky? Why do I never excel at work or get the promotion? Why has my career faltered? Why do I feel like a perennial loser?

Could it be other people have had greater achievements than you because they have more self-discipline?

If you are like me, you don't want to believe it. And I'm really good at telling myself I'm just not the self discipline kind of person. I've convinced myself self discipline is not for me.

It's time you and I embrace a new reality: Self-discipline makes the difference between high and low-achievers.

Self-discipline can:

- Turn an average ball player into a great one.
- Change a mediocre parent into a model parent.
- Transform a C student into an honor roll student.
- Push you out of mediocrity into stardom.

But how do you get this elusive self-discipline? Here are a couple of suggestions I plan to implement in my own life.

First, set the stage for self-discipline to be easier. If you want to lose weight, not having cookies in your cabinet makes it easier to have self-discipline at home. Get an accountability partner. Set the stage for self-discipline to succeed.

Second, stop lying to yourself that you can't do it. Of course you can. But as long as you believe the lie, you won't even try. Prohibit yourself from saying, "I can't." Instead of having a cuss jar, have an "I can't" jar. Every time you tell yourself you can't, throw a dollar in the jar.

Third, accept the reality that it's not going to be easy. The word "discipline" carries the idea of "punishment." No wonder we back away from the idea of self-punishment. But it's a reminder. It will not be easy. Here's the good news: Even though it is hard you can do it!

Fourth, start small. My level of self-discipline is pretty low. It makes sense to start small. Build on small successes and move on to harder self discipline challenges.

If you want to rise above mediocrity, try self-discipline. It just might change your life.

Apply this to your life:

1. In what area of life do you most need to start applying self-discipline?

2. How can you set the stage for self-discipline to be easier?

3. What specific small steps can you take to get the self-discipline process started?

# CHAPTER 21: DISCIPLINE NOT DESIRE DETERMINES OUR DESTINY

Have you read *The Secret*? This book teaches the Law of Attraction which means if you think about something long enough you will get it. Put this idea into book form and you could sell a million copies! And that's what author Rhonda Byrne did. The total sales of this book now exceed 19 million. And why not? Everyone would like to believe that if you want a new car all you need to do is imagine the car and "poof" it magically appears.

This is not a new idea. Decades earlier Napoleon Hill wrote *Think and Grow Rich*. His book carried the same message: If you want something keep thinking about it. His book sold more than 70 million copies. It is still a popular book as evidenced by the fact that I once sold a first edition of this title online for $650.

People want to believe that if you desire something all you need to do is think about it and that "thing" will be drawn into your life.

What an absurd idea! We know better! But get honest. Don't you and I often live by this idea more than we want to admit? We have a dream list of what we want:

   - a new car
   - a better job
   - a pay raise
   - a dream vacation
   - a slimmer body
   - a better relationship with our kids

So what's your plan for these dreams? Be honest. Too often all we do is think about them, hoping they become a reality.

But this item from *Tom's List* reminds us it is NOT enough to think about these things. Dreaming and thinking are important. But life has taught each of us that it takes more than dreaming. The real secret to obtaining what you want is found in discipline. And there's the problem. That's why the "just think about it" authors became millionaires. We hate the word discipline so much we will spend money on a book that teaches us to dream and it will happen.

I have an idea. Let's make peace with the word "discipline." Let's sit in an imaginary circle and smoke the peace pipe. What would happen in your life if you embraced discipline instead of avoiding it? I'm convinced your dreams would start to come true.

Discipline is the doorway you must walk through to transform your life.

To make friends with discipline, change how you think of it. When I think of discipline I think of dieting and being deprived. I'm guessing your idea of discipline is tied in with a negative experience. Here's what I'm going to do to start embracing discipline: I'm going to view it as a friend instead of an enemy. I'm going to think of the future results instead of the present pain. And if I want something bad enough, I can become friends with anybody or anything to get it.

So what about you? Are you going to make discipline your friend?

Apply this to your life:

1. When you think of the traits of friendship, write down what comes to your mind.

2. Think through how to apply these traits into your concept of discipline.

# CHAPTER 22: WHAT YOU DO EVERY DAY MATTERS MORE THAN WHAT YOU DO ONCE IN A WHILE

Have you ever opened your big mouth and later wished at that moment you'd been struck with laryngitis?

Several years ago I sat around the table eating with friends, all of whom were much younger than me. They started talking about their recent racing experience called "The Warrior Dash." This 5K Dash incorporated obstacles such as mud pits, fire pits, and barbed wire. As they described the agonies of the Dash in great detail, I opened my big fat mouth.

Unable to stop myself, I said, "I could do that." It was like dropping a bomb into the conversation. People laughed and rolled their eyes while mischievously eyeing my protruding belly. But the gauntlet had been thrown down. I committed myself. There would be no turning back. Or so I thought.

To prepare for the event I made a plan: Every day I would walk. And then as the weeks passed, I would make the walks longer. Instead, I walked once in a while. To compensate for walking only a couple of times a week I tried to increase the intensity of those times when I did work out. But as the Dash neared, I realized my preparation had not prepared me at all. I dropped out before the race even started.

*Tom's List* is right: What you do every day matters more than what you do once in a while. What can you do every day, that over the course of a year, will make a big difference in your life?

For example, I did the math and discovered if I stopped adding creamer to my coffee every day, at the end of a year I would lose five pounds. Not adding creamer to coffee is a little thing, but to drop five pounds is pretty significant, especially when you need to make no other changes!

What is it you can start doing daily that, at the end of a year, will bring significant dividends to your life?

What if every day you tried the following:

- Read the Bible for ten minutes?
- Stopped eating M & Ms?
- Walked for 20 minutes?
- Listened to an inspiring ebook as you commute?
- Encouraged someone?
- Wrote 200 words for the book you've been writing for five years?

Here are three reasons why doing the right thing every day, even in small doses, produces such positive results:

1. It establishes the habit of doing good things. Here's a general rule of thumb that flows out of *Tom's List*: It is far better to do a little good every day than a lot of good once in a while. Doing a little good every day establishes a habit of doing right. As you establish the daily dose of doing good, your life will start heading in a positive direction.

2. It takes big goals and breaks them down into daily chunks. I'm the kind of guy who wants to lose 30 pounds in one week. That's so unrealistic you might be laughing! But it's not unrealistic to work at controlling my eating every day knowing that in a year losing 30 pounds is a reasonable goal. All 12-step recovery programs know and preach the power of "one day at a time."

3. It gives you a continual sense of victory, a feeling of accomplishment. If you daily do the right things, even in small chunks, you can go to bed at night feeling like a winner. How long has it been since you've felt like a daily winner? And as you develop consistency in doing good things each day, your self-esteem increases.

This is a *Tom's List* commandment packed with the potential to transform your life one step at a time.

Apply this to your life:

1. Identify an area of your life that needs to change.

2. What is the one small thing you are going to start doing every day to improve this area of your life?

# CHAPTER 23: LIFE IS A SERIES
# OF DAILY HABITS

Thirty-four years ago I taught myself to program a computer. And what I learned is at the heart of this commandment from *Tom's List*.

The Commodore VIC-20 sat in front of me while I punched in the letters so my son Matt and I could play Donkey Barrel. It took a long time to type in all the lines of Basic code from the instruction sheet. While messing around with punching in lines of code, I learned about sub-routines. These small, self-contained loops performed a specific function in the game. For example, one sub-routine might be lines of code that reset the game when all the "lives" were used up. When you string all the sub-routines together you had a complete game. And, you can tell by my description, programming never became my vocation!

As you go through each day, a series of sub-routines are operating in the background. These sub-routines are more often called habits. Think about it: Each day is made up of a series of habits. Life is a series of habits.

All you need to do to prove this to yourself is think of the first 30 minutes of each day. I'm guessing the half hours of each morning are almost identical. Why? Because you are operating with a series of habits (sub-routines) in place. If you dissect the rest of the day you will see other small habits kicking into operation, propelling you through the day.

In 1984 Eliyahu Goldratt wrote a novel called *The Goal*. Through a fictionalized story of a faltering manufacturing company it teaches the importance of Systems Thinking. In the manufacturing process, there are many departments; for example sub-assembly, assembly, sanding, and painting. And each department can be called a sub-routine of the larger process. Systems Thinking says the effectiveness of the entire process can never rise above the effectiveness of the weakest department in the system. If one department can only produce 2,000 units a day, but other departments can do 4,000 a day, the company is limited to producing only 2,000 units in a day.

I'm thinking this concept of Systems Thinking can be transferred to our daily lives. And the small habits of the day are like departments that manufacture your day. When you go to bed at night, you've manufactured a day. What has shaped the quality of the product? What has limited your effectiveness? The answer is your weakest habit.

I've never read a book on this subject. And I've never heard anyone talk about this concept. But I think there is something to it.

Let's recap:

A day is pieced together by small habits that often run unnoticed in the background.

At the end of the day, you have produced another page in your life story.

The quality and effectiveness of the day are limited to the effectiveness of your weakest habit.

The takeaway lesson is clear. Find your weakest habit and make it a better habit or get rid of it.

Apply this to your life:

1. Think through your day. What is the one thing you do that has the biggest negative impact on your day? Find that one habit and change it or kill it.

2. Do you start the day wrong? What if you began the day reading the Bible or other uplifting material instead of the news?

3. Do you look in the mirror each morning and remind yourself how old you are getting? Get a large copy of *Time's* "Man/Woman" of the year cover, cut out the center, and tape it to the mirror.

4. Are you in the habit of opening the refrigerator door every time you walk by? Tape a picture of how you looked 30 pounds ago next to the handle.

5. Is there a person at work who regularly puts you in a bad mood? Decide you will do everything possible to avoid him or her.

# CHAPTER 24: GENEROSITY: HE WHO REFRESHES OTHERS WILL HIMSELF BE REFRESHED

It was an odd way to spend Christmas Eve. But when I awoke, God had a crazy mission for me to carry out. And at the end of the day I had experienced the highlight of my year.

Here was the God-given plan: stand out on the street corner and hand out $5 bills. Trust me, this is not something I would have thought of on my own. It is not in my nature to be generous, especially to strangers. At first I rejected the idea as being too crazy. People would laugh. And, after all, it was my money! Why give away money to people I didn't know?

Against my better judgment, I got a big piece of cardboard and wrote "Merry Christmas . . . Free Money." I went to the bank and got a thick stack of fives. Placing myself on a busy street corner, feeling like a bad cartoon character, I raised my sign in the air while snow pelted me in the face. The first car came by and slowed down to read the sign. As I walked over the driver wagged his head "no" and sped away. "Whose idea was this?" I grumbled to myself.

It did not take long, however, for things to change dramatically. A few people rolled their windows down and took the $5 bill I stuffed in their face. People started to honk and wave. Traffic increased when my picture got posted on the Facebook page of the local newspaper. Some people parked their cars and walked over to me asking why I was doing what no one ever does. Several requested to have their picture taken with me. Before long I ran out of money so I went and got more. Hours later, frozen and broke, I called it a day. But I had discovered giving to others was an exhilarating experience!

When we do generous things, something happens deep down in our soul. When you give to others, in a surprising way, you are the one who gets the most out of it.

A couple of months ago, while sitting in Starbucks, I gave the barista a $10 bill with the instructions to use it to pay for the coffee drinks of the next two people. I sat and watched from my easy chair to see the reactions. The next two people came and received a free drink from this anonymous donor. But not one jumped up and down for joy. Neither recipient of my momentary generosity even smiled. And yet, I still felt good down on the inside.

These two little stories illustrate an important point about giving and generosity. The payoff isn't in the "thank you" but in the act of giving itself. It's the inner joy that springs up knowing you did something not required of you. And regardless of the response of the recipient, there is the corresponding inner joy.

What about you? Have you discovered the raw and pure joy of giving to others? I challenge you to be generous today. Give something away. Shock someone with your unexpected generosity. Give money. Or give a smile. Why not give someone your place in line at the grocery store? I assure you, you will get more out of it than the one who receives.

Today, what can you do to experience the personal joy of generosity?

Apply this to your life:

1. Think through your plans for the day. Where will you go? Who will you see?

2. In those settings, what act of generosity could you perform?

3. Do at least one act of generosity today and discover for yourself the joy of giving.

# CHAPTER 25: LORD, GIVE ME THE WISDOM TO KNOW THE RIGHT THINGS TO DO AND THE COURAGE TO DO THEM

This chapter is for those facing major life decisions. If you are not up to reading and thinking about critical hinge points in your life, stop and come back to this one another day.

It will soon be three years ago since I faced a critical hinge point. I had been the pastor of my church nearly ten years but sensed my ministry coming to a close. I had no idea what to do. But it became clear God wanted me to resign. Once I knew what to do I needed the courage to do it. This presented a challenge because I loved the church and I had no other job lined up. One of the most difficult moments in my life happened when I resigned to my church board.

Have you ever had a time in your life when you didn't know what to do? And when you found out what to do you lacked the courage to do it? We all face times like that in our lives. Maybe you are even facing one of those moments right now. Have you been thinking about:

> - Major career issues?
> - Struggles in your marriage?
> - Downsizing your house?
> - The broken relationship with your son or daughter?
> - Suicide?
> - How to handle your feelings of utter despair?

In these tough life moments there is good news. And the good news is this: If you don't know what to do, God does. In those big league life moments our ignorance of what to do doesn't mean there is no answer. There is an answer. There is a way out. A solution exists. God knows what it is but you don't, at least not yet.

This is why this commandment is a prayer. "Lord, give me." The answers to life's toughest problems are found outside of ourselves. Since this is a prayer, we are reminded we need to pray. Maybe you are not a religious person. That's fine. God still cares about your needs. Give prayer a try. And if you've never prayed, let me help you. Start like this: "Hi God.

Please help me." It really is simple. And when you've had your say, stop and listen as you watch for God to work. You might feel impressed to do or say a certain thing. Or you might see something amazing happen to clear up your uncertainty.

Not only does wisdom come from God, but courage does also. It's one thing to know what to do but a different thing to do it. Too many people, once they know what to do, pull back and fail to do the right thing. Don't be like that. And if you find yourself being afraid, just remember: Without fear, there can be no courage. It is only when we know what to do, and push through the fear of doing it, that our lives can improve.

I take tremendous comfort in knowing God has it all figured out. He will give you and me the needed wisdom and courage to face the major challenges in our lives.

Simple. Powerful. Profound.

Will you let God help you?

Apply this to your life:

1. Make a list of the major life challenges you face.

2. Prayer is just talking to God. Try it. Talk to Him as you would someone seated next to you.

3. Go ahead. Ask Him for the wisdom you need and the courage to live as you should.

# CHAPTER 26: CHARACTER IS THE WILL TO DO WHAT IS RIGHT EVEN WHEN IT IS HARD

*char·ac·ter* ˈkerəktər/*noun*
*The mental and moral qualities distinctive to an individual.*
*"running away was not in keeping with her character"*

Quick. Picture a bow.

What came to mind? Did you see a curved stringed weapon used to shoot arrows? Or did you picture a yellow ribbon neatly tied on top of a present? Maybe you saw a man in a suit face a lady bending toward her at the waist? And some will have pictured the front end of a ship. When you are reading there is only one way to tell what the word means. It all depends on the context in which the word is used.

This commandment focuses on a word that needs context to make the meaning clear. It's the word "character." When you think of character, what comes to mind? Do you think of a person who is a bit eccentric and of whom you say, "He's a real character?" Or do you think of someone who possesses inner strength and does the right thing?

One use of the word "character" carries a negative feel. But the other use is the opposite; it carries a positive feel. What makes the difference? The difference is how we live in the context of life. And the distinguishing hallmark of a person who has character is someone who does what is right no matter what. You will recognize a person of character when you see someone who does the right thing even when it is the hard thing.

Too often when presented with the need to make a decision we ask the wrong question: "What's the easiest thing to do?" We've learned water runs downhill without any effort. Dump a bucket of water on the ground and you know it will seek the path of least resistance. Too many people live life using water running downhill as their model. When it's decision time, they seek the path of least resistance. They seek the easy path. Why not? Why bother? Why make the effort?

But at this stage of life, we've all learned the path of least resistance is rarely the best path. A person who lacks character seeks the easiest path. For example, they:

- Fail to go to a person they've wronged and apologize.
- Make a mistake at work but won't go to the boss and confess.
- Remain in a job but is only coasting to get a paycheck.
- Never pursue a true passion because it means sacrifice.
- Don't make the commitment to complete an important task because it turned out to be more difficult than they first thought.

Here's an idea. When you hear your brain say, "That's too hard," pay close attention. This might be a signal indicating this is what you are supposed to do. And what you do in the context of life, will give you the answer.

So are you a character or do you have character?

A person of character embraces the hard things in life knowing it produces the best things in life.

Apply this to your life:

1. What hard things in life are you ignoring that could make you a better person? *Stop getting orange slices limit wine*

2. Think through the benefits of tackling the hard things.

3. Decide to take on these challenging places in your life knowing it builds character.

*gossiping*

# CHAPTER 27: TALENT AND DETERMINATION DETERMINE YOUR POTENTIAL, CHARACTER DETERMINES YOUR LEGACY

While speaking to a group of people I held a large rock in my hands over a pop can. As my hands supported it in the air I described the potential energy of the rock. Trust me. The 65-pound rock had plenty of potential! But as long as my hands were in place it only had potential energy. Then, I removed my hands. The potential energy turned into kinetic energy. BAM! The rock slammed into the can and crushed it.

We tend to admire potential. "Oh, he has so much potential," says the proud parent. And often what we mean is he has talent and a certain amount of determination.

In our culture, we admire talent. How often have you looked at someone and felt in awe of his or her talent? And the TV show *America's Got Talent* is a hit for good reason. We know talent when we see it. Talent breeds admiration.

But we know talent is not enough to make our mark in this world. We've often been told it also takes determination. How many times has an encouraging friend said, "You've got to stick with it!" We know to really make it in this world we will encounter setbacks and roadblocks. Determination is a necessary key to success.

When you have talent and determination you, like the rock being held in the air, have potential. You will make a mark in your world with talent and an "I'll never give up" attitude. There will be a few accomplishments along the way. But to realize your full potential, to turn your potential energy into a crushing legacy of kinetic energy, you must work on your character.

When we work on our character, we are acknowledging we are in it for the long haul. A pastor who resigned from his church after two years confided in me, "I feel I've left a legacy." In two years? Not likely. Legacy is the resounding impact we leave behind over a lifetime.

This commandment reminds us that legacy is ultimately shaped by our character. Why? Because our character, the distinctive collection of our moral and mental qualities, determines our course over the long haul. You can have great talent but leave behind a broken life. It's possible to even have talent and great determination and not leave behind the kind of legacy you really want.

Character is the major determining factor as to whether we leave behind a negative legacy or a positive legacy.

Character development is an important subject not to be trivialized by a quick five-point list in this chapter. Do whatever it takes to develop your character.

Apply this to your life:

1. Go to the Amazon website and search for a book on the subject of character development. Purchase one with a large number of positive reviews. Read the book with the purpose of finding at least three ways to build your character.

2. If you are religious, I suggest you take seriously the *Bible* verse found in Matthew 6:33 that teaches us to seek God first and ourselves second. When you put God first everything else tends to fall into place.

# CHAPTER 28: PARENTING IS MORE CAUGHT THAN TAUGHT

As a young parent, I wanted to teach my kids Matthew and Emily how to grow up to be good citizens and followers of God. I had the idea my goal could be accomplished by looking for teachable moments where I could deliver my wise insights. Wrong. Since then, I've been reminded many times of the real way kids learn from a parent. They learn best by example.

I once took a preaching class in seminary from an accomplished minister. He led us through a couple of textbooks. I heard him lecture for many hours about technique. He talked of his preaching experiences across the years. I learned a lot from him. But one day he preached in chapel. As he preached I watched him deliver the message. I marveled at his timing, the delivery, the eye contact that captured my attention. In his 30-minute sermon I learned as much as I did in his semester-long class. Some things are better caught than taught.

Being a parent, or a grandparent, is like that. It's more caught than taught.

Your kids and grandkids watch and learn from your actions. And this is true if they are three or 39 years of age. They watch and learn. They might listen to the little life lessons you teach them in those teachable moments, but they are learning most by watching how you live your life.

Are your kids raised and you feel a sense of guilt over your lack of parenting skills? (I think most parents, including myself, beat themselves up later in life because they feel inadequate as a parent.) Do you look back and realize you did not set the perfect example?

Just a minute. Not so fast. Let me tell you a quick story.

My dad's parenting skills went into the negative column. As an alcoholic, a smoker, and an abuser of illegal prescription drugs he set a horrible example. I saw and experienced many negative things growing up with him as a father. But guess what? I learned by his example. I remember with clarity as a young teen promising myself I would not live my life as he did. I learned by his negative example. And to this day I've never smoked, or tasted alcohol, or abused any kind of drug. Dad taught me well.

So if your kids are grown and you beat yourself up over not setting the best example, cut yourself some slack. As adults they are making their own decisions. There is nothing to be gained by revisiting your past parental mistakes and heaping guilt on yourself.

The best thing you can do as a parent is live your life NOW in such a way that you are a positive influence in their life. Even if your adult kids live 1,000 miles away, they are still watching how you live. Make the decision to set a positive example for them.

You cannot undo the past but you can influence a child's life tomorrow by how you live today.

If you are a grandparent, you have the privilege of a potential do over. Learn from your past failures. Live your life now in a way to be a positive influence on your grandchildren.

Apply this to your life:

1. What's the most valuable life lesson you've learned from a parent by watching how he or she lived?

2. Did you pass this lesson on to your children?

3. What is the most important lesson you are now passing on to your children or grandchildren?

4. Identify one lesson that needs to be taught and live your life in such a way that they get it.

# CHAPTER 29: PARENTING: WHO YOU ARE MATTERS MORE THAN WHAT YOU DO

I can't explain how it works. Maybe it doesn't work. But I've seen plenty of evidence to suggest it might. What am I talking about? It's the idea that a dog takes on the traits of its owners. Have you ever noticed how often this is true?

People with every hair in place and a fussy temperament walk carefully groomed dogs with a temperament matching their owners'. People who strut around looking for a fight walk the neighborhood with a pair of wild-eyed blue-nosed pit bulls. Owners of golden retrievers stroll the sidewalk with their own tail wagging while flashing a continual smile.

Somehow, so the theory goes, the traits of the owner are transferred to the dog. It's like some sort of strange magic.

The same can be said for being a parent. (And we may as well remember, being a parent never ends. *Tom's List* is for every parent regardless of age.) As a parent you are passing traits on to your kids. When it comes to parenting, who you are matters more than what you do.

Parents ought to look for teachable moments. Yes, spend time talking to your kids about how they ought to be as a person. But talk only goes so far. At a deeper level, a magical level, your kids are picking up your traits and making them their own. I'm not sure how this happens. But when you give it some thought you will recognize it is true.

Not long ago a picture appeared on Facebook of a young mother and her three-year old daughter. The picture had been cropped to show their faces side by side. They looked like the same person but at different ages. We can point to the science of genetics to explain the similarities. There is nothing we can do to change it.

But when it comes to the traits we pass down to our kids and grandkids, there is something we can do about it. We can work on ourselves until OUR traits are ones we want to pass on to them.

Here's a couple of suggestions for every parent and grandparent who wants to make a positive impact on the following generations.

First, examine your own life and identify the most negative trait. You can identify it by asking this simple question: "What is it about my life that I hope my kids never copy?" Maybe your questions come back with answers resembling these: I'm too stingy, I hold grudges, I fail to show my love, I trust no one, or I am always grouchy.

Second, once you have identified your least desirable trait, do whatever you can to attack it. Deal with it. Work hard on your life to clean it up. Read a book. Get counseling. Confide in a friend. Do whatever it takes get rid of that one trait you do not want to see reflected in your kids.

And when you've changed one harmful trait go to work on another. If your kids are three or 33, they are worth it. Who you are is more important than what you do.

Apply this to your life:

1. What positive traits have your kids and grandkids picked up from you? Keep living your life to reinforce those traits.

2. Do you see any negative traits that you've passed down to them? Take the appropriate steps in your life to change these traits.

# CHAPTER 30: YOUR CHILD'S CHARACTER HINGES ON THE TRAITS YOU EXHIBIT AS A PARENT

There are times I don't want to face the truth. Over the years, I've discovered I'm pretty inventive when it comes to shifting blame from myself to others or something else.

For example, my entire life I've struggled with my weight. During many of those years I had convinced myself the extra weight was not my fault. Those unnecessary pounds were a result of how my parents raised me, my genetic makeup, too much stress, or being too busy.

All of these things may factor into the problem. But the only hope for weight loss came when I stopped making excuses and took personal responsibility.

The same is true when we think about the impact of our own traits as parents upon the lives of our kids. There are many factors that forge the character of your kids. But none is more important than the traits you exhibit to them. I've heard many parents who have tried to dodge their responsibility in this area. If their child runs into trouble, the parents often blame the school or the church or the child's group of friends.

Here's the truth each parent must face: How YOU live your life is the single greatest influence on the development of your child's character.

This is a fact which holds true whether your child is young or old. Regardless of their age, your child watches how you live your life.

Last week I heard of a church staff person who was released from their position by the senior pastor. The reasons behind the action seemed thin and driven by insecurities of the senior pastor. The staff person posted a statement on Facebook about what had happened. In the statement, the staff person urged the church folk to get behind the pastor who had made the decision and called him a "good man."

Not surprisingly, the three grown children of the staff person made a comment to the post. And each child talked about the character of their parent. The actions of the parent revealed character. And those actions impacted each child, continuing to forge their own character.

We've all known parents who seemed to do everything right but the child made bad decisions. It's true we cannot live our lives beating ourselves up for the bad decisions our kids make. There are no guarantees in parenting. But when it comes to forging the character of our children, we must take responsibility to live our own lives above reproach.

As parents we dare not forget that our character, exhibited by our daily actions, continues to impact our children. It is the single greatest influence we can have upon their lives.

Today live your life in such a way that it will build character in your kids.

Apply this to your life:

1. Which of your personal characteristics do you see in your children or grandchildren?

2. What positive things can you do to model character in the lives of your children or grandchildren?

# CHAPTER 31: NO AMOUNT OF SUCCESS AT WORK CAN MAKE UP FOR YOUR FAILURE AT HOME

Do you remember the birth of your first child? I do. The nurses whisked my wife down the hall into some magical room where the miracle of birth took place. Meanwhile I paced the floor in another not-so-magical room. In this waiting room I waited and worried. But family surrounded me. Some lived too far away to be there but the ones who waited and worried gave me comfort and strength.

Do you remember the first funeral you ever attended? I do. My great-grandfather lay sleeping in a box at the end of a big room filled with the sights and smells of flowers. I trembled as a relative clasped my hand and led me toward the box so I could peer inside. At my young age I didn't understand. But I will never forget the large crowd of family members coming together to support one another.

From cradle to grave there is nothing more important than family.

But as we grow up we often forget the primacy of family. Life becomes more about "me" than it does about "us." And as the years roll by, parents and grandparents become consumed with building a career and making money. Building a career and making money is great but too often it is done at the expense of the family.

One of the greatest tragedies in our society is how often the family is sacrificed on the altar of material success.

You know what I'm talking about. One or both of the parents have sights set on being a success in their chosen career.

If it takes working 60 hours a week and ignoring the family, so be it.

If it means never taking a family vacation because of a busy schedule, you tell yourself they will understand.

If you need to work two jobs to pay the bills as you claw your way to the top, the kids will need to just suck it up.

If the pressure at work makes you a tyrant at home, you try to convince yourself it's for the good of the family.

Will you stop for a moment and remind yourself that no success at work will make up for your failure at home?

As parents, our HIGHEST calling is not to pour our lives into our work but to pour our lives into our family.

The newborn baby is surrounded by family members as they peer into the bassinet. Someone observes, "Oh, what a cute baby." And at the funeral home a family member peers into the casket and says, "He looks so good." Can I be honest? The newborn is wrinkly and has a smushed face. The person in the casket doesn't look good, they look dead. But that's what family does. They look at each other and believe the best, in the best of times and in the most challenging of times.

I need my family. So do you. It's time to work harder on your family than on your career.

Apply this to your life:

1. Remind yourself that nothing is more important than family. Nothing. Take a few moments and evaluate where family is on your priority list.

2. Schedule time for your family. When you schedule family time, keep the appointment knowing it is sacred.

3. Determine to work on your family relationships until family is your No. 1 priority. It will take hard work but it will be worth the effort.

4. Never believe the lie that says it is too late for your family. You cannot undo the past. But with effort you can begin to improve your relationship with family.

# CHAPTER 32: THE GREATEST GIFT I CAN GIVE MY KIDS IS A HEALTHY MARRIAGE

What's the greatest gift you ever received from your parents? It's a tough question. My parents lived paycheck to paycheck. Money seemed to be in short supply. Maybe that's why my brother and I were stunned the day Dad took us outside and pulled two new bikes out of the backend of the beat-up station wagon. It wasn't our birthday or Christmas. But to this day I consider it the best gift they ever gave me.

Most parents love to give gifts to their kids. If you're a parent, you know the deep thrill you receive when your son or daughter opens a really cool gift. When they light up, you light up. Funny how that works.

*Tom's List* makes a bold statement. It says the best gift you can give your kids is a healthy marriage.

What? Giving your kids a healthy marriage in the home they grow up in is better than:

- A paid for college education?
- Season tickets to the Chicago Bears?
- A hot new car?
- A European vacation?

It's a bold statement. But I believe it is a true statement. There is no greater gift you can give your kids than to raise them in a home where the marriage is healthy.

Your kids deserve to grow up in a home where they feel safe. They need to see parents modeling what a couple in love looks like. They need to learn by observation how a man in love treats a woman. They need to see how a woman treats the man she loves. They need to learn what it means to be a parent so when it comes time for them to raise a family, they have a foundation to build on.

Not only were my parents unable to give me expensive gifts, they were unable to give us kids the gift of a healthy marriage. My earliest memories consist of hearing them fight as I cried myself to sleep. One of the happiest days of my life was the day I left home and headed off to college.

But my experience as a child made me determined to raise my kids up in a loving environment where they could see what a healthy marriage looked like. It's a goal I'm still working on.

If your marriage is struggling, get to work on it. Even if your kids are raised they still watch and learn from you about marriage. Do whatever it takes to improve your marriage. Read a book. Get counseling. Talk to your pastor. On purpose, fall in love with each other again.

Do you get it? This isn't just about you and your spouse. It's about your kids and their kids and the generations to follow.

Apply this to your life:

1. What rough spots in your marriage need attention?

2. Consider attending a marriage enrichment seminar to improve your marriage.

# CHAPTER 33: MARRIAGE: FIND THE MOST GENEROUS EXPLANATION FOR EACH OTHER'S BEHAVIOR AND BELIEVE IT

Elvis Presley saved the best for last. In his career he had 17 number one hit singles. The last of the bunch had the title "Suspicious Minds." The song, written by Mark James, focused on a real-life personal marriage struggle dealing with trust.

As the song made clear, it's difficult to build a strong relationship in the environment of suspicion. When we wonder why our spouse said or did something and imagine the worst-case scenario, we are destroying the marriage.

This commandment reminds us of the importance of giving your spouse the benefit of the doubt. But don't stop there. Go ahead and believe the best possible cause for his or her actions. If you are going to make up a story of why your spouse did something, why not make up one where they are doing something good?

I once knew a couple who lived exactly the opposite of giving each other the benefit of the doubt. They assumed their partner did and said things to inflict pain and hurt. If you picked a movie title to describe their marriage it would be *Conspiracy Theory*. A friend of mine once remarked the couple lived at sword points. I'm not going to be surprised if I discover their marriage didn't last.

But what if your spouse is really doing something wrong? What if they are having an affair? What if they are trying to push your buttons? What if? Remind yourself time always reveals truth. The truth will come out. But until then decide you are going to believe the best about the actions of your spouse.

This is by no means a new idea. This truth has been around for centuries. It is even found in the number one best-selling book in the history of the world: the *Bible*.

Paul, a follower of Jesus, writes a letter to a church in Corinth, Greece. The church is struggling with many internal issues. As Paul writes he includes a section dealing with loving each other. In that section there is this line: "Love always looks for the best."

Our challenge is to always look for the best in our spouse. Sometimes it's difficult. There are times when we are angry and want to find a reason to lash out. But wait! Give your spouse the benefit of the doubt.

When you abandon your conspiracy theories and suspicious mind, your marriage becomes stronger.

Apply this to your life:

1. What are some areas in which you've struggled to give your spouse the benefit of the doubt?

2. What can you do to build trust in those areas? Start with communicating your difficulty with your spouse. Work together to build trust.

3. Make the decision you will believe the best until truth proves you wrong.

# CHAPTER 34: WISE PEOPLE BUILD THEIR LIVES AROUND WHAT IS ETERNAL AND SQUEEZE WHAT IS TEMPORARY

I met a man who had documented every day of his life for the past 20 years. With great pride he bragged of being able to pick any date in those 20 years, look at a journal entry, and tell me what he did on that particular day. His journal collection spanned a large shelf. When I asked him why he went to all the trouble of making those records, he shrugged his shoulders as if to say he had no idea.

But I know why he did it. He's trying to hang on to each day. We all have this feeling on the inside that the clock is ticking. Before we know it, life will end. It's all gonna be over. And, to borrow a picture from Tony Campolo, they're going to take our body out to the cemetery, throw dirt in our face, and go back to the church to eat potato salad.

Here's where I scratch my head. If we all know life is temporary, why do we spend so much time and energy buying a boat? A fancy car? A vacation home? A fifth wheel? Sure, on some level I get it. We all want to enjoy our life. But here's the trap: We spend our life working hard to pay for things that don't last and ignore building our lives for eternity.

Don't fall into the trap of focusing so much on the things of life today that you fail to prepare for eternity.

Even if you are a reader who doesn't believe in God or heaven, you still ought to stop and think about what's really important. Wise people build for eternity. Everyone who dies leaves behind a legacy. Are you concerned about your legacy? Does it matter how you are remembered? If I believed the grave is the end, I would work hard on my legacy. I would want people to remember my life and be inspired. In death we leave part of us behind. And the piece I leave behind ought to guide the generations to follow. Don't live just for today! Don't fall into the trap of sacrificing tomorrow's legacy on the altar of materialism.

And if you fall into the religious camp, you too know the truth of these words. We are building for the future. We will leave behind a legacy but we also are headed for a bright future. Our hope is in Christ. And we plan on living forever in a place called the new heaven and new earth. Let's live today in such a way to prepare for eternity.

In the early 20th century, missionaries went to far-off, third-world countries to take their religious message. Part of the preparation focused on packing their coffin. Literally. They put their few belongings inside their burial coffin. For them, turning back was not an option. These missionaries had figured out the importance of building their lives around the eternal.

Wise people build their lives around what is eternal and squeeze what is temporary.

Apply this to your life:

1. Why do you think it is so easy to become confused and believe temporary things are the most important?

2. What temporary thing should you squeeze so you can focus on the important things that last?

3. Answer this question: As I examine my life, do I see it is focused on things that really matter? If not, study your life and make the needed changes.

# CHAPTER 35: LEADERSHIP: GET THE RIGHT PEOPLE ON THE BUS

One of the most powerful leadership lessons is the importance of getting the right people on the bus. And this lesson applies even beyond your job. It helps us in every arena where people gather together to accomplish a shared goal.

This leadership lesson comes from *Good to Great* by Jim Collins. He recognized that a company, group, club, church, and any other group you can name becomes more effective with the right people in leadership.

Why is this so important? What happens when the wrong people are on the bus? Here are three quick examples.

First, the wrong people will try to take you in the wrong direction. They envision the organization as heading in the wrong direction. When that happens, they will do whatever possible to move the bus toward a different goal or destination.

Second, the wrong person takes the joy out of the journey. This kind of person yips and yaps about every real and imaginary bump in the road. They are negative, filled with criticism, and deflate the morale of everyone on the bus.

Third, the wrong person simply doesn't produce. They are not a productive member of the team. They might be nice people, but they are a drain on the organization because they consume more from the organization than they produce.

There are many other examples of the wrong kind of people to have on the bus but I've mentioned these for a reason. In 35 years of leadership I've had to fire three people. Only three. And the ones I fired fit the examples I've just mentioned. They were the wrong people to have on my bus. I tried to work with them and, from my point of view, I did everything possible to help them. But when it remained clear they were on the wrong bus I had to let them go. And in each situation, the organization ultimately became stronger once the people got off the bus.

What about the people on your bus? Do they contribute to the forward motion of the team and organization? Or do they slow down or stop progress?

Once you identify the wrong people, make every effort to help them become the right people. Work with them. Encourage them. Mentor them. But if you do not see progress, you may need to let them go. No one said it would be easy. But it's worth it to get the right people on the bus.

Apply this to your life:

1. Have you ever been on the right bus? What did it feel like to be part of a unified team or organization?

2. Have you identified any people in your life who are on the wrong bus? What can you do to help?

3. If these people do not respond, be prepared to part ways with them.

# CHAPTER 36: WHAT GETS MEASURED AND REWARDED GETS DONE

I have a new thought on the leadership principle of "what gets measured and rewarded gets done." As a leader, you cannot delegate and assume a task will be completed. Good leadership demands follow up. And one of the best ways to followup is to measure and celebrate the progress.

If you've ever been in a leadership role, you know exactly how this works. You ask an employee, a volunteer at church, or a family member to do something. "Oh sure. I'll get right on that," says the one receiving the instructions. You walk away assuming your role is over. But too often, you find out the hard way that they make little, if any, progress on the task.

This leadership principle applies to every situation where you are leading someone else. But here's my new thought. What if we applied this leadership principle to ourselves?

There are many times when I've pledged to myself to complete a task and failed to complete it. How about you? How many times have you done the following:

- started to read a book but never finished?
- made a New Year's resolution which crashed and burned within 30 days?
- started a diet but bailed out in 48 hours?
- resolved to mend a broken relationship but it just never happened?
- went back to school to finish your degree but dropped out?

What if you took the leadership principle and applied it directly to your own life? What if you started to measure and reward your progress in the tasks you've assigned yourself? I'm certain you would see an increase in the completion of your goals and projects.

To measure your progress, you need to start by setting definite goals. Many people, including myself, have proclaimed they are writing a book. Great! How's that going? The majority of aspiring authors would confess it's not going well. But what if you assigned specific writing goals? If you set a goal of writing 500 words every day, you would have a way to measure progress. Any task that is important to you can be broken down into measurable goals.

If this is the only truth you get out of reading any part of *Tom's List* to this point, it is enough to turn your life around. This simple idea of setting goals and measuring progress can be a game changer.

As you make progress in achieving your goals, don't forget to celebrate. Reward yourself with whatever provides motivation. Celebrating the small milestones helps to keep you chugging away so you can reach your ultimate goal.

Apply this to your life:

1. When you set goals, write beside each one the reward you will give yourself when you reach it.

2. What are some small rewards you can dangle next to the goals you have set?

# CHAPTER 37: PLAY TO YOUR STRENGTHS AND DELEGATE YOUR WEAKNESSES

Have you ever made root beer? One day I gave it a shot. I gathered the ingredients and placed them in a gallon glass jug with the metal lid screwed down tightly as the recipe instructed. I placed the concoction under the kitchen sink in a cabinet with great expectations. Several hours later, during a *Seinfeld* rerun, I heard what sounded like a cannon blast from the kitchen. Running to the kitchen, I saw the cabinet doors had blown open. Shards of glass littered the floor. And a strange, brown liquid ran like a polluted river towards me. Then and there I decided to never again make another batch of root beer. This seemed best left to the experts.

You are really good at some things. Celebrate those things. Work on your strengths to make them even stronger. Playing to your strengths is a strategy we naturally embrace.

But there are a few things that are outside of your skill set. We celebrate what we do well but tend to ignore what we don't do well. Big mistake. If you ignore those areas in your job, or family, or education, or retirement that you cannot do well, it might come back to bite you.

Take a pastor for example. Most pastors are strong in some areas but weak in others. Think of the pastor who is strong in preaching but weak in building close relationships with others. This pastor loves to preach but hates to do counseling or get involved in the personal lives of others. What should he or she do? To ignore the problem will only create a larger problem. People will feel neglected and overlooked. Here's the answer: The pastor should find someone who is good in the area of their own personal weakness. As a team there will be success.

In what areas of your personal or professional life are you weak? Regardless of your current status in life, this is a good question to ask. Think of this question until you come up with an answer.

As a retiree, are you unable to generate an active social life? You ought to consider joining a few clubs that will generate a list of social activities for you.

As a grandparent, do you struggle with social media leaving you less connected with your grandchildren? Find someone who will come into your home and set up the technology you need. Wouldn't you love to see the faces of your grandkids as you talk to them from 2,000 miles away?

As a wannabe world traveler who isn't good at planning, what do you do? Stay home and read *National Geographic*? No. You need to pick up the phone and call a travel agent. Let the experts put it all together for you.

As a struggling single parent who isn't sure how to raise kids by yourself, do you keep limping along? Nope. You should consider talking to a single parent who navigates those waters with success. They will be happy to give you pointers.

It's doubtful if anyone can journey through life without the help of others. Some people, those who struggle and often fail, keep trying on their own to succeed. But those who have the sense to reach out to others for help often enjoy success.

Apply this to your life:

1. Identify your strengths. What are you good at? In what area of life do people give you compliments? Build on those strengths

2. In what areas of life do you struggle? Once you've made a list, find someone who can help you. Reach out to them. Stay focused on your strengths.

# CHAPTER 38: STUDY TOP PERFORMERS AND MODEL THEIR HABITS

In 1938, Esphyr Slobodkina wrote a classic children's book called *Caps for Sale* based on the saying, "Monkey See, Monkey Do". A cap peddler wears his inventory on his head with the hats stacked on top of each other. He falls asleep under a tree. When he wakes all of his caps are gone except the one on his head. When he stands up, he sees monkeys sitting in the tree each wearing one of his caps. The peddler screams at them and shakes his fist. The monkeys imitate his actions. In disgust the peddler throws his cap on the ground. Like magic, the monkeys imitate the action and throw their caps at his feet.

"Monkey See, Monkey Do."

When we want to improve our lives, it is natural to look at the leaders in the field in which we want to excel.

If you want to become a great leader, you look to the writings of Zig Ziglar or John Maxwell.

If you want to become a great pastor, you will keep your eyes on Andy Stanley.

If you want to become debt-free and wise in how to handle money, you look to Dave Ramsey.

If you want to start a business and become a billionaire, Mark Zuckerberg might grab your attention.

There is much to be learned by studying the leaders in the field in which you want to improve. But there's a danger. Too often, we fall into the "Monkey See, Monkey Do" mentality. We decide we will simply copy what they do.

Years ago the church growth movement sprung up. It taught pastors that the ultimate good could be found in filling every seat on Sunday morning. To make this a reality, pastors attended conferences to learn from pastors who had grown large churches. At the end of the conference you could purchase a step-by-step guide on how you too could grow a huge church. But the church growth movement crashed and burned. Why? Because it tried to implement a "Monkey See, Monkey Do" mentality.

Copying what someone does often fails to produce results. Your context is different. You are working in a different environment with different people. There are factors unique to your situation at play. Copying what someone does sets you up for disappointment and failure.

If you've decided to copy the behavior of an expert, you've missed the mark. It is far better to study the habits of leaders. It is the difference between "doing" and "being." Great leaders do what they do because of who they are. And they've become who they are through the habits they have acquired.

When we learn to instill the habits of the leaders we admire, we become more like them. Once you've discovered the leaders in your field and determined their habits, try to build those habits into your own life. It will take time and hard work. But did you really expect to find a shortcut on your way to becoming the best in your field?

Apply this to your life:

1. Identify leaders in the field in which you need improvement.

2. What lessons do they teach you?

3. This next step is important: How will you apply those truths in your own context?

# CHAPTER 39: SELF-RELIANCE: I WON THE PROBLEM, I OWN THE SOLUTION

"You screwed it up. You fix it."

This is the sage counseling advice few people ever have the courage to give someone who is struggling with issues in his or her life. And some-times those words would be inappropriate. But once in a while that's the advice people need to embrace. They created the problem and they should fix it.

But in our culture, we have become experts at blaming others. You know how this goes. People say, "It's not my fault:

- You don't know what my dad did to me."
- You don't know how she treated me."
- I was born with a short fuse."
- You'll never understand what I went through."
- The government rules forced me into doing it."
- She pushed me."
- He made me mad."

We have become so good at making excuses, when we hear ourselves make one up, we believe it. And here's the beauty of excuse making. If it isn't my fault, I feel no responsibility to make it better. Excuse making fosters the victim mentality. Instead of looking for answers we look for sympathy and understanding.

I'm in favor of sympathy and understanding, but I am much more inter-ested in finding a solution. And as long as I'm finding excuses it's difficult to find solutions.

If you want to make improvements in your life, take responsibility for the problem and go find the solution. Stop wallowing in self-pity. The excuses you give to your friends and yourself are wearing thin. Stop it. Enough is enough. It's time to get on with life.

You may not have caused every problem in your life. Things happened to you that were out of your control. For example, it wasn't my fault Dad molested me as a young kid. But here's the thing. We are responsible for our response. And it is our response that either creates problems or creates solutions.

Here's an idea: Pick one area in your life where you struggle the most. Do you need to lose weight? Are you struggling in your marriage? Have you been unemployed for longer than a month? Do you have a child who won't talk to you? Are you and your neighbor at war? Pick one of these areas where you really struggle.

Now, take a few moments and make a list of reasons (excuses) why this is an issue. Get all the excuses out on paper. Then, take a deep breath and mark a huge X through all of them. At the bottom of the page write these words: "It's my fault and I'm going to fix this." You are now free from excuses and free to find solutions.

"BUT IT'S NOT THAT EASY!" Did you say that? Sounds like another excuse to me. None of this is easy. But it is the path to becoming a better person.

I dare you to try it. Stop making excuses. Go and make solutions.

Apply this to your life:

1. What problem areas in life do you find yourself making excuses?

2. Look at the list and figure out how to stop making excuses and start making progress.

# CHAPTER 40: LEADERS ARE READERS: WE ARE WHAT WE READ

The final hurdle for students in the master's degree program from which I graduated was the oral comprehensive exam conducted by three professors. Poor performance meant a delay in graduation. For me all went well until this question, "Who said, 'you are what you eat'?" Failing to come up with the correct answer, the professor asking the penetrating question informed me the answer was "Feuerbach." At that moment, I thought, "Who really cares?"

But the question makes a good point. What goes in determines what comes out. This is true of the food we eat, the software we load into the computer, and the stuff we put into our brains.

Leaders must be readers of quality books, blogs, and articles.

We all know people who have stopped reading and stopped growing. A colleague once informed me he heard our boss brag about how he had not read a book in more than a year. No wonder working under him was like a continual bad scene from the movie *Groundhog Day*.

Failure to read robs you of new ideas and ways to improve your life.

My friend Tom, who left behind this list of 50 commandments, succeeded partly because of his commitment to read. In the first chapter of *Tom's List*, I told you of his goal to read one new book each week. In ten years he would have read more than 500 books. Imagine the information and inspiration gleaned from those books!

One of the reasons *Tom's List* exists is because of the books he read. He took the theme of the most impactful books which he read and distilled it into a single sentence. Over the years he collected 50 great truths based on his reading. You and I are the fortunate recipients of his reading and thinking.

When was the last time you read a book? Let me encourage you to become a reader. Even if you struggle with reading, the more you read, the more you will improve. Choose your books carefully. There are only so many books you can read over the course of your life. The huge selection of books demands you make good choices when reading.

As you read, to become a leader in your field, start your own list. Distill the most helpful truth from each book you read into a sentence. Collect them and live by them. If you do this, maybe someday after you are gone your loved ones will discover your list. And that discovery may change their lives.

Apply this to your life:

1. Identify a subject area in which you need to do more reading.

2. Make every effort to read the best blog or book available.

3. Generate a reading list and work through it.

4. What book are you going to start reading?

Good to Great

# CHAPTER 41: LEADERSHIP = INFLUENCE

Substitute teaching is not for the faint-hearted. When you walk into the classroom and see the eager students mentally drawing a red bullseye on your forehead, it is disconcerting.

One class where I substitute taught started with no problems. But as the period dragged on things went downhill. Assessing the situation, I realized the challenge. One of the students decided to push the envelope. Others followed his example. He was the leader and became the primary influencer over the other kids. He set the tone and they started to follow.

Leadership is like that. It is the ability to influence others. Right away a few people will claim no leadership ability. But those few people are wrong. Everyone has a certain level of influence over another. There is someone in your world who follows your lead.

With leadership comes responsibility. Not too many authors write about the responsibility of leadership. But I think it is a critical component. As a leader you have a clear responsibility to lead people in the right direction.

I pulled the student with leadership qualities aside and told him I'd been watching him. I let him know he had leadership qualities. But there was a problem. His influence led the other kids down the wrong path. I told him he had a responsibility to lead his classmates in the right direction. I asked for his help. From that moment to the end of the class, he used his leadership abilities to maintain order in the classroom.

The Pied Piper of Hamelin was a rat catcher hired by a town to lure rats away with his magic pipe. After disposing of the rats, the town refused payment. To exact revenge, the Pied Piper played and led the children out of town. There are differing versions of the fairy tale, but most of them end with the townspeople never seeing the children again. The Pied Piper had great influence, but he chose to use it negatively.

As you think of your influence, remind yourself of the inherent responsibility of leadership. You can be a good influence or a bad influence. The choice is yours to make. To become a good leader, you must first look at yourself. You must determine to influence others in a positive direction.

Who watches what you do? Who is going to be influenced by your actions? At this stage in my life I'm thinking more and more of my influence over my grandchildren. I have a responsibility to lead them in the right direction. The responsibility is mine. The choice is clear. I must be careful of my actions and how I live because I know I am influencing others.

The story of the Pied Piper ended with tragedy. The children all died. This little fairy tale reminds us of the tragic consequences of using our influence in a negative way. Decide now you will use your influence only in positive ways.

You are being watched. You are being followed. Lead them in a positive direction.

Apply this to your life:

1. Who has been the biggest positive influence in your life? Jason

2. What was it about his or her life that beckoned you to follow them?
   Deep Faith, Concern for others, problem

3. Can you use those characteristics to lead others? solver

# CHAPTER 42: SPEED OF THE LEADER = SPEED OF THE TEAM

Have you ever worked in a factory on the assembly line? The entire assembly line can only go as fast as the slowest step in the manufacturing process. The same is true when it comes to leading any group. The speed of the leader determines the speed of the team.

This is not a news flash. We all know if the star basketball player has a good game, the team wins. If the new principal has it all together, the entire school moves forward. And if the department at work has a fireball leading the way, there is improvement.

But what might be new to you is to apply this principle to yourself. In earlier chapters of *Tom's List*, you were reminded you are a leader. You have a sphere of people, few or many, over whom you exert influence. Now take this thinking a little further. As a leader, you set the tone. You help determine the speed of the team.

The first challenge in this principle is to own this truth: We are so accustomed to blaming someone else.

"Management is holding us back."

"It's the fault of the union."

"I wish my spouse would get her act together."

"What we really need is a new mission statement."

"If my mother-in-law would just stay out of it."

Instead of blaming everyone else, take a deep breath and realize you hold the key. Do not shy away from this truth. For the sake of everyone on the team, embrace this truth.

Do you get it? Did you take responsibility? You determine the speed of the team. As John Maxwell said, "Everything rises or falls on leadership." When those you lead fail to move forward, a good leader looks in the mirror first to determine the problem.

Perhaps as you think about your ability to influence, you will pat yourself on the back. Maybe those who follow you are making progress. Congratulations! The team is moving forward thanks to your efforts. But there is also the possibility you are holding the team back. If so, don't ignore this revelation but do something about it. Lead, follow, or become a greeter at Walmart.

Not long ago, this truth hit home in a personal way. For nearly 30 years I was in a leadership position. Toward the end of those years I felt worn out. I assessed the situation and realized the organization was faltering because of me. I tried all sorts of things to correct the situation. Nothing worked. I tendered my resignation. Lead, follow, or become a greeter at Walmart. Your speed determines the speed of the team.

Apply this to your life:

1. Think of those who follow you. Are you moving them forward? Or are you slowing them down?

2. What can you do to recharge your batteries and increase your speed?

# CHAPTER 43: YOU BECOME LIKE THE FIVE PEOPLE YOU ASSOCIATE WITH THE MOST

Not long ago I went with a friend to spot a moose in the wild. We had no luck but I saw some stunning scenery. We were on several obscure service roads that took us high up into the mountains. Far below us, you could see beautiful Lake Coeur d'Alene. There were no lakes on the top of the mountain. Why? Because water runs downhill and seeks the lowest common level.

There is a warning for us.

You become like the five people you associate with the most.

In the arena of sports I'm a loser but I did pretty good at table tennis. I loved to win. Crushing an opponent gave me great satisfaction. But here's what I discovered. The more I played opponents I could easily crush, the more my game went downhill. But if I dared play opponents who could crush me, my game improved dramatically.

Think about the five people you hang out with the most. Are those people dragging you down to their level or are you rising up to their level? Does your association with them make you a better person? Heads up. Who you spend time with, really does impact your life: for your detriment or your betterment.

You need people in your life who will challenge you and make you better by association.

Make a list of the five people with whom you spend the most time. With butt-ugly honesty answer this question about each person: "Is he making me a better person or is he pulling me down in the wrong direction?" If you spend lots of time with someone who is a negative influence on you, make the decision to spend less time with them.

Do you want to become more successful in your field? Do you need to be encouraged? Are you lacking confidence? Think through the qualities you need more of in your life.

Now go and find people you can hang out with who have those qualities. The Internet has made this easy.

You might decide you need more courage. If that's true, hang out with Sir Winston Churchill. Study his life. Read his books.

If you need to be inspired and motivated, make friends with the writings of Dale Carnegie or Norman Vincent Peale.

Join a Facebook group dedicated to the quality you need more of in your life and find a friend.

You might know someone at work who outperforms you. Why not take them out for coffee with the goal of making a new friend?

You have the power to choose the five people with whom you hang out with the most. It is important to remember those people are either helping you or hurting you. Sure, we need to help people who are less fortunate than we. Don't stop doing that. But why not seek out people who will make a positive impact on your life?

A couple of years ago I drove into Yellowstone National Park through the northeast entrance along Beartooth Highway. The magnificent road escorted me to an elevation of 10,000 feet. Guess what I saw at those higher elevations? I saw a couple of small lakes shimmering in the sunlight. There are times when water stays at a higher level. Make it your goal to associate with people who help you to stay on top.

Apply this to your life:

1. Do you have a friend right now who is making you a better person by association?

2. If you have any friends who bring you down, consider spending less time with them.

3. Make a list of five friends you need to make. This could be a person or their writings.

# CHAPTER 44: THE SIGNATURE OF YOUR WORK AND VITALITY OF YOUR NETWORK WILL DETERMINE YOUR PROFESSIONAL FATE

Many people struggle to find success at work. Regardless of the job or industry, many people never rise to the level called success. When this happens, the one struggling is forced to ask the questions, "What's wrong? Why am I having such a difficult time?"

Here's the easy road most answers go down: "It's because of circumstances beyond my control." This is the idea of looking for answers outside of ourselves that we contribute to our lack of success. Check out the following:

> - "The economy is hurting my industry and no one is succeeding."
> - "My coworker has it out for me and he's working behind the scenes to bring me down."
> - "My boss is an idiot."
> - "My company hasn't a clue on what they are doing."

The other road, the less traveled road, is to admit a lack of success is your own fault. Those who blame others conclude there's nothing they can do and keep on living with the frustration resulting from a lack of success. But those who take the hard road by admitting they are responsible for their own fate can then do something about it.

For those willing to admit their failure at work is an internal problem, *Tom's List* suggests two ways to find success.

First, focus on the quality of your work. You will become known by the quality of what you produce.

Take a hard look at what you are doing. Do you meet or exceed standards? Are you giving it your best efforts? Are you producing or just getting by? Find ways to improve. Do whatever it takes to improve your contribution to the company.

Second, focus on the vitality of your network. In our technology-driven culture, you must be connected.

With the flexing muscle of social media, it is more important to be well-connected than talented. When it comes to your job, you can have everything going for you but if you are not connected, success will be elusive. The new status symbols of connectedness are the number of Twitter followers and Facebook likes on your business page. But numbers are only numbers. You need to work at making real connections.

When it comes to determining your personal success, which road will you go down? The road of blaming outside circumstances is a road of frustration leading to a dead end. But the road that travels inward looking for solutions, while difficult, will lead to success.

William Ernest Henley wrote these inspiring lines in his famous poem *Invictus*:

"It matters not how strait the gate,
How charged with punishments the scroll,
I am the master of my fate:
I am the captain of my soul."

If our discussion was theological in nature, I might argue against Henley. But when it comes to success at work he is spot on.

Go. Take the road less traveled. Make today a success.

Apply this to your life:

1. What's the hardest thing about finding success at your work?

2. What is the one thing you can do to improve the quality of your work?

3. With whom can you connect to improve what you do?

# CHAPTER 45: LIFE IS 10% WHAT HAPPENS TO ME AND 90% HOW I CHOOSE TO RESPOND TO IT

His first business failed. The Traf-O-Data, a device designed to read traffic tapes and process the data, didn't even work. No wonder the company failed. But Bill Gates didn't let the failure stop him. He points to his company woes as preparatory in making his next company, Microsoft, a success.

At the age of 13, surfer Bethany Hamilton had her arm bitten off by a shark. And I mean the arm was gone all the way up to her shoulder. But one month later she climbed back on her surfboard. Two short years later, she won first place in her division of the NSSA National Championships.

She was born into poverty to a single teenage mom. She grew up in an inner city neighborhood. Molested as a child, she became pregnant at 14; her son died in infancy. And yet Oprah Winfrey went on to become one of the richest and most influential women in the world.

Here's the point. Every one of these people experienced adversity. No one would've blamed them if they had raised the white flag of surrender and stopped trying. But they didn't. They used the things that happened to them as springboards to success.

Too many people use the adverse circumstances in their lives as excuses for failure. People who live like this become overwhelmed by their circumstances. But *Tom's List* reminds us life is 10% what happens to us and 90% how you choose to respond. If you and I could embrace this fact, we would stop making excuses and start looking for ways to succeed.

How do you turn adversity into fodder for success? The answer is found in a key technique used in the martial art called judo. The idea is to use the force of your opponent and redirect it. The bully who chases you will go flying if you know how to redirect his energy.

Use the potentially crippling energies of failure, bad luck, and the actions of people and redirect them. Let those things stir you up and motivate you to try harder and work smarter. DON'T surrender or use those things as excuses for failure.

Apply this to your life:

1. Think of an important area in your life where the possibility of success is fading. Instead of giving up, make a list of the excuses you are using for not achieving in this area.

2. Now do some judo. Look at each excuse NOT as a barrier keeping you from success, but as a source of energy that you need to redirect.

3. Stop making excuses. Anyone can do that. Be different. Go get yourself a black belt in turning adversity into victory. And then you will know the joy of success in the face of adversity.

# CHAPTER 46: REFUSAL TO TAKE RISKS MAKES FOR A LIFE OF MEDIOCRITY AT BEST

Do you always play it safe, refusing to take any risks? Are you the person who sticks with the familiar even when it's boring? Have you turned down a job opportunity because it felt too risky? When you think of transitioning out of your current career, does your blood pressure spike?

Here's what I've learned: Refusal to take risks makes for a boring life of mediocrity.

When it comes to flying, I am King Coward. My cowardice is legendary in my circle of close friends. During takeoff and landing I often put a jacket over my head. And while cowering and trembling in the darkness, I've been known to have tears stream down my face in fear.

Even though I am a flying coward I've made the decision to not let fear keep me out of the air. As much as I loathe flying, my desire to experience new places and cultures is stronger. If I had not taken the risk of flying, I never would have:

> - stood in the Roman Coliseum and marveled at its history.
> - trekked through the mysterious city of Petra in Jordan, one of the Seven Wonders of the ancient world.
> - helped construct a building for missionaries in the jungle town of Macas, Ecuador.
> - sailed the Sea of Galilee and walking the streets of Jerusalem.
> - slept beside a smoking volcano in Guatemala.

Life is all about taking risks. The truth is you take risks every day. When you get out of bed, you risk falling. Climbing behind the wheel of your car and pulling into traffic is a huge risk. Even getting into an elevator and pushing the button is risky business.

When you dare to take risks, the payoff is potentially huge. Unless you are willing to take a risk, you will never get a better job, see another country, or rejoice at victory in a hard-fought battle. Failure to take a risk results in a boring life of mediocrity.

There is no benefit in risk-taking just to take a risk. Decide to take calculated risks. I despise roller coasters and all amusement park rides. Every year I read of accidents at theme parks where someone falls out of the sky or gets stuck at the top of the Terror Twister. But I am 100% certain those things will never happen to me. Why? Because I will never get on those rides.

Pick your risks carefully. Make sure the risk is worth the reward. But when you see the reward, lay the risk aside and go for it. It's time to ditch the boredom and breathe the air of adventure.

Apply this to your life:

1. What are you missing out on because you refuse to take a risk? Think of some concrete examples.

2. Do a risk versus reward analysis. Do the rewards outweigh the risks?

3. Decide on one major risk you will take in the next 30 days.

4. After you take the risk, enjoy your reward.

# CHAPTER 47: BUSINESS OWNER MENTALITY: ALWAYS TRY TO MAKE DECISIONS AS IF YOU OWNED THE BUSINESS

Have you ever been tempted to think you are going through life alone and you can make up your own rules? This is not something anyone wakes up one morning and decides on a whim. Instead, it is a lifestyle we gradually adopt. And we often see it exemplified in the workplace. It is there we are tempted to take advantage of the company we work for. We have the idea it's OK to cut corners or take office supplies home for our own use.

But *Tom's List* reminds us we should have a business owner mentality. How would we treat the company if we owned it? I suspect we would no longer cut corners or pilfer office supplies.

There is, however, a larger truth behind having a business owner mentality. It's this: you are part of a bigger whole. And how you act impacts the whole.

In an earlier chapter, I mentioned my zip-line adventure in Guatemala. In the truck headed up the mountain with me was another person inflicted with the same temporary insanity. I soon discovered he was a brilliant expert in quantum physics. Taking advantage of the moment I asked, "Of all the lessons you've learned about quantum physics, what is the most important?" He thought for a moment and replied, "I've learned that everything is connected."

Everything is connected. You are part of a greater whole. In some way your actions, for good or bad, impacts the lives of those around you.

John Donne is right. No man is an island. We do not travel through our lives all alone. And even when we proclaim life is "all about me" we lie to ourselves. Life is all about us.

- When you slight your company, you hurt the company.
- When you fail to live to full potential, you are cheating all of us.
- The shame and pain of homeless veterans belongs to all of us.
- When you get a promotion at work, we should all rejoice.

- The agonizing plight of someone else around the world is our plight.
- When I announce I've lost another three pounds, you should do the happy dance.
- When you put new shutters on your windows, those who drive by should enjoy the upgraded beauty.

Here's the bottom line. Each of us needs to be careful to live our life to its fullest potential. It's not about you. It's about us. We are in this together.

Apply this to your life:

1. Is this how you live your life?

2. Identify some actions you've made that had a negative impact on those around you. If you are still making decisions that hurt others take some time to evaluate those actions.

3. List the positive benefits of living your life by remembering we are all connected.

# CHAPTER 48: TWO KEYS TO LEADERSHIP: LEADERS CAST BOLD VISIONS AND LEADERS TAKE BIG RISKS

I'm old enough to remember the days when owning a car meant you carried two keys. One key opened the trunk, the other started the car. An effective leader must understand there are two keys to leadership. The first is a bold vision to put in the trunk; the other is taking big risks to move the vision down the road. A leader who takes big risks without vision is a fool. The leader who casts bold vision without taking big risks is also a fool. Both keys are needed.

Don't give into the temptation to skip over this principle because you do not feel like a leader. We are all leaders. Some are leaders because of employment and others simply because of who they are. If you are skeptical let me remind you of the simple definition of leadership: "Leadership is influence." Almost every person on the planet exerts some sort of influence over someone else. Even as you watch toddlers in a pre-kindergarten class you will see this truth in action.

If you have ever been to Disneyland, you know it's an incredible experience. This magical kingdom did not happen magically, but grew over the years under the bold leadership of Walt Disney. I once read he would meet with his board and propose new projects to expand the wonderful world of Disney. But here's the thing. He would not pursue his own project ideas unless everyone said it could not be done! Disney knew the importance of casting bold visions and taking big risks.

If you are going to be a leader who lives to your fullest potential, you must have bold vision and take big risks.

Garry, a regular reader of my blog, has won my admiration. He comments often on my articles. In those comments, he casts a bold vision and is prepared to take risks. Even though he's past 50 years of age he's going back to school to become an art teacher. That's a bold vision involving some risk. But he's going to succeed. I applaud him! And in the end he will make a terrific impact on his students.

Do you see how important it is to have both keys? It's one thing to have a big dream. But without taking risks it will remain only a dream.

Be bold. What is it that gets your motor running? Take a risk and make it happen.

Apply this to your life:

1. What do you dream about? What vision of your future keeps you awake at night? What dream did you carry for years but it died? Go find those dreams. If they are dead, revive them. But grab the biggest dream rolling around in your head.

2. Now make a list of what it takes to turn your dream into reality. Sure, it involves risk. But that's the point. Bold dreams deserve big risks!

3. So here you go. Fill in the blank: My biggest dream for my own life is

_____.

# CHAPTER 49: NEGOTIATION: THERE IS ONE KEY PRINCIPLE: THE PERSON WHO HAS MORE OPTIONS HAS MORE POWER

Have you ever negotiated but failed? You might not think of yourself of as a negotiator but think again. Have you ever done the following:

- Asked your boss for a raise?
- Tried to get your grandson to take school more seriously?
- Talked your spouse into agreeing to join you in YOUR dream vacation?
- Convinced the car salesman to give you a discount?

If you've answered "yes" to any of these, you are a negotiator. It's one thing to be a negotiator but another to be a good negotiator.

I grew up back in the TV era of three channels. Not long ago I subscribed to cable TV, with hundreds of channels to choose from. Over the years, the cost of cable TV rose sharply. Like many people, I called my cable company and negotiated a lower monthly fee. At the end of the negotiations, I stood tall because I knew there were other options. When it comes to negotiations, the person who has more options has the most power.

Before you enter into any negotiations, take time to explore ALL options. Think of the example of television. You can ditch cable and stream programs through Netflix or Hulu. Sling TV is another good option. And guess what? They make great indoor HD antennas. Or here's another idea: Give up TV and see how much more time you have for life.

Explore all your options. List them from most desirable to the least. Try to go for the most desirable. If that doesn't work, go to the next. Decide ahead of time which outcome you most prefer. Even if you end up going down through the list, you still end up with a desirable outcome.

When you enter into negotiations, keep your options handy. The ultimate power is knowing you do not need to settle for a deal that doesn't make you happy. You can always walk away.

It is a great feeling to confidently enter negotiations with your list of options with high expectations. Just remember, this is not the time to bluff. You are not playing an inconsequential game of friendly poker. The stakes are high. No bluffing. You must be committed to acting upon your preferred option.

Have you ever seen a parent negotiate with his or her toddler in the grocery store? You know the routine. The little darling in the shopping cart makes a scene. The parental negotiations start: "If you don't stop that we are going home this very minute." Of course this does not achieve the desired results. The parent then starts counting, "One, two, threeeee . . ." What usually happens next? Nothing, absolutely nothing. The parent was bluffing and now the child has an even stronger position of power in the relationship.

If you want power in negotiating, examine your options and be prepared to follow the best course of action for your life.

Apply this to your life:

1. Identify three areas in your life where negotiations need to happen.

2. Use the suggestions above and start negotiating.

# CHAPTER 50: THE GOOD THINGS IN LIFE ARE OFTEN THE ENEMY OF THE BEST THINGS IN LIFE

Are you in love with the word "good"? When someone asks, "How are you?" is the reply "good"? Do you love "good" weather? Was yesterday a "good" day for you? Do you live in a "good" house in a "good" neighborhood and drive a "good" car?

Too often the good things in life become the enemy of the best things in life.

Have you ever noticed you can buy a book on Amazon for one penny? Why would sellers do that? The answer is they received $3.99 from the customer for shipping. If the seller can ship for $2.99, he makes one dollar for each sale. That sounds good. Do the math. If he sold 100 books each day using these numbers he would make $100 each day. Making $500 each week selling 500 books for a penny is good.

It's good but not great. Why? By the time you found books, listed them, and shipped them there would be no time for anything else. A better approach is to sell just five books for $100 each. That would be great! Now you have more time to think and plan on how to grow your little business. The good is no longer the enemy of the best.

Here's a profound but simple truth: Good is good but it ain't great.

If you're content with good you'll never achieve great. You'll never lead the field, stand above the crowd, lead the way, or excel.

When you settle for good you have set your sights too low. You have crawled into bed with mediocrity. And mediocrity is a seductive voice that poisons passion and productivity.

My friend Tom, the one who compiled these 50 commandments for living, is a spectacular example. His goal of reading one book each week wasn't good, it was extraordinary. And because he didn't settle for the good, but reached for the best, we have these 50 truths to live by. He has impacted many by his refusal to settle for good.

Think about your life. What good things are keeping you from doing the best things? What good things in your life gobble up the precious resources of time and energy? What would happen if you raised your sights from good to great?

Apply this to your life:

1. For the next 30 days, refuse to allow the good things in life to keep you from the best things in life. During those 30 days do three things:

> - Examine your life for good things that can become great. Here's a helpful question: What one thing would help my life the most by shifting from good to great?
> - Find a way to move from good to great. Think. Explore. Pray. Often the move from good to great is achieved by a simple tweak.
> - Consider reading *Good to Great* by Jim Collins or the easier to read book *An Enemy Called Average* by John Mason.

2. You can settle for good but why not go for the best? Decide you will strive for greatness.

# EPILOGUE: TOP TEN RANDOM LESSONS LEARNED AFTER WRITING *TOM'S LIST*

Here are the top ten random lessons I've learned after writing on the 50 commandments on *Tom's List*.

1. Tom was really smart as evidenced by the quality of his list. I love the deep wisdom contained in the list he left behind. Each commandment challenged me to be a better person.

2. Reading pays off. I believe people who make a difference in their world are people who read. Tom's life serves as an example. As a result, I've increased the number of books I'm reading.

3. Life is too short. I can hardly believe Tom is gone; passing away before turning 60. As I worked through the list I often thought of how we all need to make each day count.

4. If you consistently work at a big task it will get done. Making a commitment to write on each of the 50 commandments was a stretch. But I found that as long as I kept the commitment to write each week a big task became manageable.

5. Everyone will leave a legacy. The only question is what will it be? Tom touched so many lives. People still remember his impact. Working through his list has forced me to focus on my own personal legacy.

6. With effort, anyone can become a better person. *Tom's List* is all about becoming proactive and taking charge of your life. Too many people allow life to pass by without challenging themselves and remain mired in mediocrity.

7. A life is enriched by the number of quality friends you have. In the fall of 2016, I will attend my 40-year college class reunion. It was there I met Tom and a group of guys who became my best friends. My life has been richer because of these quality friends.

8. Writing is hard work. To write and post every week isn't easy. How many people do you know who have said, "I'm writing a book" but never finish? I've gained a deep admiration for people who write.

9. A publicly declared goal is more likely to be accomplished. I'm great at starting things but often struggle to complete them. As you think of your goals for the next twelve months, be bold and declare them publicly on Facebook or to your family.

10. True friends are rare and more valuable than any earthly treasure. Don't take your real friends for granted. Stay in touch. Enjoy them while you still have them.

# ABOUT THE AUTHOR

Dr. Randall K. Hartman, D.Min., M.Div., B.S., is a Baby Boomer riding the wave of transition from a long established career to an encore career.

After serving 30 years as a successful minister, he discovered a passion for challenging Boomers to make their post-career lives the best part of their journey. Instead of sliding into a retirement phase of life, he believes it is far better to ReFIRE your life. Using his writing, speaking, and coaching skills he helps people transition into their most vibrant and meaningful years.

As an independent contractor for New Church Specialties he also travels the country helping churches through times of transition.

Dr. Hartman earned a doctor of ministry degree from Grace Theological Seminary. He graduated cum laude with a master of divinity degree from Nazarene Theological Seminary. He received a bachelor of science in Business Administration from Olivet Nazarene University.

To learn more about Dr. Randall K. Hartman and the ReFIRE process, visit randallhartman.com.